Gilberto Fachetti Silvestre
Camila Villa Nova Ramalho
Davi Amaral Hibner

Accessibility and personality rights

Gilberto Fachetti Silvestre
Camila Villa Nova Ramalho
Davi Amaral Hibner

Accessibility and personality rights

Material and procedural issues

ScienciaScripts

Imprint

Any brand names and product names mentioned in this book are subject to trademark, brand or patent protection and are trademarks or registered trademarks of their respective holders. The use of brand names, product names, common names, trade names, product descriptions etc. even without a particular marking in this work is in no way to be construed to mean that such names may be regarded as unrestricted in respect of trademark and brand protection legislation and could thus be used by anyone.

Cover image: www.ingimage.com

This book is a translation from the original published under ISBN 978-613-9-72538-0.

Publisher:
Sciencia Scripts
is a trademark of
Dodo Books Indian Ocean Ltd. and OmniScriptum S.R.L publishing group

120 High Road, East Finchley, London, N2 9ED, United Kingdom
Str. Armeneasca 28/1, office 1, Chisinau MD-2012, Republic of Moldova, Europe
Printed at: see last page
ISBN: 978-620-7-92283-3

SUMMARY

CHAPTER 1	**5**
CHAPTER 2	**11**
CHAPTER 3	**19**
CHAPTER 4	**26**
CHAPTER 5	**36**
CHAPTER 6	**49**

PRESENTATION

This book is the overall result of one of the studies carried out in my Research Group *"Challenges of the Process: impacts of the Civil Procedure Code on the civil legal system"*, linked to the Postgraduate Programme in Law - Master's in Procedural Law, at the Federal University of Espírito Santo (UFES), Brazil. The research, divided into three phases, involved researchers from the undergraduate, master's and scientific initiation programmes funded by the Brazilian National Council for Scientific and Technological Development (CNPq).

This is a study of some of the changes brought about by Law No. 13.146/2015 - the Brazilian Law for the Inclusion of People with Disabilities (Statute of People with Disabilities), with a focus on the thesis of the existence of moral damage resulting from inaccessibility.

The Brazilian Law for the Inclusion of People with Disabilities brought several changes to the Brazilian Civil Code in order to consider people with disabilities fully capable of exercising all acts of civil life and thus protect them through the freedom granted to them.

This study looks at the historical construction of the legal treatment of people with disabilities, and its main focus is accessibility as a right of the personality. It thus seeks to demonstrate that inaccessibility generates moral damage and gives rise to due civil reparation.

Accessibility should not be seen as a mere ideological banner for protecting the rights of a minority. This issue deserves serious treatment and must be guaranteed the concreteness so necessary for the full exercise of freedom by people with physical disabilities who have their locomotion reduced or impaired.

Freedom of movement is the first step towards independence and autonomous living, so dear to people by their very nature. And society must stand in solidarity with this cause.

My special thanks go to the editorial team of *Derecho PUCP - Revista de la Faculdad de Derecho of the Pontificia Universidad Católica del Peru,* which was the first outlet to offer us the opportunity to publish the first phase of the research (Vol. 80, pp. 9-31, 2018). I would also like to thank the *Argumentum journal* of the University of Marília, Brazil, which also gave us the opportunity to publish the second phase of the research (Vol. 18, pp. 731-758, 2017).

Finally, my sincere thanks to *Editorial Académica Española,* who kindly invited us and gave us the opportunity to publicise this research in other countries and regions.

Vitória, Espírito Santo, Brazil, November 2018.

Prof Dr Gilberto Fachetti Silvestre Federal University of Espírito Santo (UFES) Postgraduate Law Programme E-mail: gilberto.silvestre@ufes.br www.direito.ufes.br

INTRODUCTION

Social transformations in the treatment of people with disabilities led to a legislative process of creating various guarantees, rights and guidelines for the inclusion of people with disabilities. From "disabled" to "people with disabilities", they were put on an equal footing with other people in the social context. Duties were also established for federal entities, society and private individuals to protect these individuals.

The national and international standards created - which cover various areas such as labour, education, health, social security and assistance, tax benefits and others - have as their primary objective the inclusion of people with disabilities, enabling them to exercise citizenship on an equal basis with others.

In the case of Brazil, 2015 saw the advent of the Brazilian Law for the Inclusion of Persons with Disabilities - Statute of Persons with Disabilities (Law No. 13.146/2015), which regulates the Convention on the Rights of Persons with Disabilities and its Optional Protocol, both of the United Nations (UN). The LBI consolidated all the legislation previously created in order to specifically address issues essential to the protection of individuals with disabilities.

An example of the impact of the LBI on the legal system was the alteration and abrogation of various provisions of the Civil Code, the main ones relating to the civil capacity of people with disabilities, so that, currently, mere disability, whether physical or mental, does not entail incapacity to exercise any acts of civil life, which is confirmed by the list of examples in art. 6º of the new Statute, which states that disability does not affect a person's full civil capacity.

In addition, the new law sought to take a different approach to the protection afforded to such people, namely the idea that their dignity should be protected through the freedom granted to them and, furthermore, that freedom can only be achieved if society offers adequate conditions for inclusion, through the elimination of barriers that prevent the possibility of effective participation[1] .

Data from the World Health Organisation (WHO) from 2011 reveals that 1 billion people live with a disability, which corresponds to every 7th person in the world[2] .

In Brazil, the 2010 Census, released by the Brazilian Institute of Geography and Statistics (IBGE), shows that 45.6 million people declared having at least one type of disability, which corresponds to 23.9 per cent of the Brazilian population. Of this total, 84.4 per cent live in urban areas, and 15.6 per cent in rural areas[3] .

The Brazilian Law on the Inclusion of People with Disabilities has enshrined various rights for people with disabilities, establishing various rules on fundamental rights and also providing an entire Title (Title III) specifically to deal with the right to accessibility.

Based on these transformations, it emerged that accessibility was treated in the LBI as a right of the personality and is intended to fulfil the purpose of equality between all people, without discrimination of any kind, and of freedom and autonomy.

Personality rights are those powers and legal situations that protect natural persons in their fundamental aspects, namely the psychosomatic (physical), spiritual (moral) and intellectual (intellectual). These rights protect the person in what is most essential to them, ensuring the realisation of their human dignity.

By elevating accessibility to a personality right, the legal system demonstrates the close relationship between the elimination of barriers and the realisation of the dignity of people with disabilities.

Injury to an off-balance sheet right generates compensable moral damage. *In* this sense, the thesis defended here is that *inaccessibility generates moral damage.* In order to reach these conclusions, bibliographical research was carried out in order to understand personality rights in a broad sense, thus providing theoretical

---

[1] MENEZES, Joyceane Bezerra de; MENEZES, Herika Janaynna Bezerra de; MENEZES, Abraão Bezerra de. The approach to disability in the face of the expansion of human rights. In: *Revista de Direitos e Garantias Fundamentais,* 17(2), 2016, pp. 551-572.

[2] Available at: https://nacoesunidas.org/acao/pessoas-com-deficiencia/. Accessed 16 Nov. 2018.

[3] Available at: https://ww2.ibge.gov.br/home/estatistica/populacao/censo2010/. Accessed 16 Nov. 2018.

support for the hypothesis raised. It also sought to confirm the inclusion of accessibility as a personality right by researching court judgements, which demonstrated, based on specific cases, how the issue has been addressed by some Brazilian courts. From this, it was possible to prove the viability of the thesis that inaccessibility gives rise to compensation for moral damage.

Furthermore, civil liability today is based not only on the obligation to pay compensation, but also on the protection of rights via specific protection. For this reason, it was possible to formulate arguments about the full application of specific personality remedies (inhibitory, injunctive, restorative and reintegrative), in order to force the violator of the right to accessibility to make the necessary efforts to eliminate barriers against people with disabilities or reduced mobility.

The main aim of this research is not to encourage the "trivialisation of compensation" and the "moral damage industry". The aim is to present the great importance that accessibility has for the full realisation of the dignity of people who have difficulties with locomotion and perception of their surroundings, and who therefore encounter obstacles (often tiny, but which are major barriers for them) to exercising their freedom and autonomy.

Compensation for this special type of moral damage can encourage the necessary accessibility works to be carried out in environments aimed at the general public, including private properties. However, nothing replaces the process of raising social awareness of the importance of guaranteeing easy access for those whose integration into the environment is limited.

CHAPTER 1

THE GENERAL THEORY OF PERSONALITY RIGHTS

With the rise of ethical personalism in the second half of the 20th century - that is, in the post-World War II era - personality became the central value of law and the essential reason for the protection it offers. There is talk of "jushumanism", a set of values that places the human being at the centre of science, philosophy and law.

1.1. Personality as a fundamental value of law.

Today, civil personality is seen from two perspectives: *formal* and *material*[4] . From a formal perspective, personality is an attribute given by the law to certain entities so that they can be considered persons. In the material aspect, it is a value, an axiological paradigm in which the human being is the centre of the Law (jushumanisation or legal humanocentrism).

Personality is a requirement for individuals to be considered subjects of law, which allows them to: 1) be holders of legal relations; and 2) assume rights and duties in the civil sphere.

Personality, then, is the requirement for an entity - human or not, as long as it is permitted by law - to be the holder of rights and duties and to be part of legal relationships. It is what makes such an entity a *subject of law*.

On the other hand, since the second half of the 20th century, personality has become a value that is the essence of law and the protection of human dignity. In this sense, legal rules must always produce norms whose purpose and ultimate goal is to protect the personality, that is, the fundamental aspects of the person: their body (physical integrity), their spirit (moral integrity) and their intellectual capacity (intellectual integrity).

It is therefore possible to systematise what is meant by personality in the legal sphere as follows:

0 What is personality in law?	
FORMALLY	MATERIALLY
An attribute for certain entities to be considered persons (natural/physical or legal) and to be considered subjects of law and thus to be entitled to legal relationships.	0 essential value of law and the ultimate criterion for interpreting legal rules.

1.2. Personality rights.

Civil personality is much more than a formal attribute conferred by the legal system to entitle legal relations. It is, above all, a value that refers to the protection of the person. In order to protect the person, their personality, their dignity, the legal system protects a series of rights that deal with the fundamental and essential aspects of the human being: these are *personality rights*.

Personality rights are powers and legal situations designed to protect the natural (human) person in their various constitutive aspects, all considered essential to their dignity, namely: physical (right to life, physical integrity and one's own body), psychological/moral (right to image, privacy, honour and name), intellectual (right to freedom of expression and copyright) and spiritual (right to freedom of belief and religious self-determination)[5,6] .

According to Gustavo Tepedino, personality consists of the "set of characteristics and attributes of the human

---

[4] TEPEDINO, Gustavo. *Temas de Direito Civil*. 4ª ed. Rio de Janeiro: Renovar, 2008, p. 25-33. In the same vein: SCHREIBER, Anderson. *Personality rights*. 3rd ed. São Paulo: Atlas, 2014, p. 6.

person, considered as an object of protection by the legal system"[5][6][7] . In the same vein, Stea Gaetano states that personality rights aim to guarantee the fundamental reasons for life and the physical and moral development of the individual[8] .

Traditionally, five broad personality rights are known: the right to the body, the right to a name, the right to an image, the right to honour and the right to privacy. However, in the face of transformations in society and scientific and technological discoveries, new values are constantly being incorporated into the human personality, which therefore deserve protection from the legal system, despite the lack of express normative provision[9] .

Therefore, the list of personality rights provided for in the legislation that protects them is merely exemplary *(numerus apertus)* and not exhaustive *(numerus clausus),* so that other rights resulting from the human personality can and should be protected, based on the general clause protecting human dignity.

In this sense, Anderson Schreiber points out[10] :

> In other words: although the Brazilian Civil Code has only dealt with a few personality rights and has not taken care to emphasise the existence of many others in addition to those it contemplates in its articles 11 to 21, this omission does not prevent other manifestations of the human personality from being considered worthy of protection, by virtue of the direct application of article I° , III, of the Constitution.

All personality rights, in all their aspects, constitute a general clause of the integrity of the person, called *human dignity.* Integrity refers to the preservation and obligation not to harm the person in what is most essential to them. In this way, human dignity represents a general right to integrity (psychosomatic, moral and intellectual), to which corresponds a general duty of safety, which means, precisely, the duty not to harm others *(neminem Icedere).*

Antonio Junqueira de Azevedo defines the meaning of human dignity well when he locates it in the ethical-moral principle, of Christian origin, of the duty to love one's neighbour. For this reason, the author delimits the meaning of dignity to the duty to love and respect one's neighbour, which, translated into legal language, means that no one can harm the essential rights of a person[11] .

In this way, even if a certain value that is essential to the individual is not provided for by law, its protection is supported by the general clause protecting human dignity.

Articles 11 to 21 of the Brazilian Civil Code contain a *numerus apertus* list of personality rights, providing for the protection of five examples that serve as a gateway to the protection of other rights: body, name, honour, image and privacy.

However, although the Brazilian Civil Code has only dealt with some of the personality rights, other values and rights inherent to the human personality must be protected. In this sense, art. 12 of the Civil Code provides for protection against threats or injuries to "personality rights" - a term that has various meanings because it is an indeterminate legal concept - thus making it possible to protect all rights inherent to the person, including

---

[5] AMARAL, Francisco. *Civil law: introduction.* 8ª ed. Rio de Janeiro: Renovar, 2014, p. 302.
[6] FARIAS, Cristiano Chaves de; and ROSENVALD, Nelson. *Civil Law Course.* General Part and LINDB. Vol. 1. 15ª ed. Salvador: JusPodivm, 2017, pp. 221-223.
[7] TEPEDINO, Gustavo. *Temas de Direito Civil.* 4ª ed. Rio de Janeiro: Renovar, 2008, p. 29.
[8] GAETANO, Stea. The civil protection of personal rights. In: *Rivista Telemática Diritto&Diritti.* Published also in *Rivista Giurisprudenziale,* 1, 2001, p. 18.
[9] SILVESTRE, Gilberto Fachetti; HIBNER, Davi Amaral. The protection of personality rights in Brazil and Italy: material and procedural issues. In; *II International Civil Procedure Congress,* 2017, Vitória. Proceedings of the II Congress of International Civil Procedure. Vitória: UFES, 2017. v. 1. pp. 11-26
[10] SCHREIBER, Anderson. *Personality rights.* 3ª ed. São Paulo: Atlas, 2014, p. 15.
[11] AZEVEDO, Antonio Junqueira de. Legal characterisation of the dignity of the human person. In: *Quarterly Journal of Civil Law,* vol. 09. Rio de Janeiro: Padma, Jan/Mar 2002, pp. 03-23.

those that are not expressly regulated by law.

The Civil Code chose not to conceptualise and list personality rights, leaving it up to the historical moment to understand their meaning and the sense they can take on in the legal order. This historical-systematic interpretation will be made by the judge.

As can be seen, art. 12 of the Civil Code provides for a syntagm, namely the expression "personality right", the content of which is vague and imprecise, so that it is up to the judge to interpret the meaning of the expression, defining which assets, attributes or existential interests can be considered essential to the human person and therefore worthy of protection[12] .

If there is a threat or injury to personality rights, the provision establishes the consequences for the judge and the offender: stopping the threat or injury, as well as repairing the damage resulting from the transgression, without prejudice to other sanctions, which may be, for example, the removal of the offence, also provided for by law (art. 497, sole paragraph, of the CPC)[13] . Article 12 of the Civil Code therefore provides for an indeterminate legal concept. In the normative hypothesis, there is an expression of vague content, while the consequences and sanctions are pre-established by law[14] .

Thus, although the Civil Code only provides for some of the personality rights, other essential attributes of the human person can and should be recognised on the basis of Article 12, which contains an indeterminate legal concept[15] .

Gustavo Tepedino warns that personality rights cannot be limited to the legal provisions that typify them:[16] :

> Personality must be considered first and foremost as a legal value that cannot be reduced to a standard legal situation or a list of typical subjective rights, in order to effectively and efficiently protect the multiple and renewed situations in which people find themselves, wrapped up in their own varied circumstances.

In order to protect personality rights that are not provided for in Brazilian law, recourse must be had to the undetermined legal concept of art. 12 of the Civil Code or to the general clause protecting the dignity of the human person,[17] elevated to the status of foundation of the Federative Republic of Brazil and the highest value of the legal system, under the terms of art. Iº , III, of the Constitution.

Along these lines, Maria Celina Bodin de Moraes argues[18] :

> In Brazilian law, the provision in item III of art. Iº of the Constitution, which considers human dignity to be the value on which the Republic is founded, represents a true general clause protecting all the rights that radiate from the personality. Thus, in our legal system, the principle of the dignity of the human person acts as a general clause for the protection and promotion of the personality in its most diverse manifestations.

---

[12] HIBNER, Davi Amaral. *The protection of personality rights in the 2015 Code of Civil Procedure.* Master's dissertation. Postgraduate Law Programme. Federal University of Espírito Santo. Supervisor: Prof Dr Gilberto Fachetti Silvestre. Vitória, 2018-2019, Chap. 1.

[13] HIBNER, Davi Amaral. *The protection of personality rights in the 2015 Code of Civil Procedure,* ob. cit.

[14] HIBNER, Davi Amaral. *The protection of personality rights in the 2015 Code of Civil Procedure,* ob. cit.

[15] HIBNER, Davi Amaral. *The protection of personality rights in the 2015 Code of Civil Procedure,* ob. cit.

[16] TEPEDINO, Gustavo. Crisis of normative sources and legislative technique in the general part of the 2002 Civil Code. In: TEPEDINO, Gustavo (Coord.). *A parte geral do novo código civil: estudos naperspecttva civil-constitucional.* 2ª ed. Rio de Janeiro: Renovar, 2003, p. XXL

[17] HIBNER, Davi Amaral. *The protection of personality rights in the 2015 Code of Civil Procedure,* ob. cit.

[18] MORAES, Celina Maria Bodin de. *Na Medida da Pessoa Humana. Studies in civil-constitutional law.* Rio de Janeiro: Renovar, 2010, p. 128.

In a similar vein, says Francisco Amaral[19][20][21] :

[19] AMARAL, Francisco. *Civil Law: Introduction,* ob. cit.

[20] In this sense, CJF Statement no. 274, approved at the IV Civil Law Conference, states: "Statement no. 274: Art. 11: Personality rights, regulated in a non-exhaustive manner by the Civil Code, are expressions of the general clause for the protection of the human person, contained in art. I° , inc. III, of the Constitution (principle of the dignity of the human person) [...]".

[21] By way of example, although there is no specific legal provision, the Superior Court of Justice has recognised that transsexuals have the right to change their name and sex in the civil registry, regardless of whether they have undergone sexual reassignment surgery, as can be seen from the following judgment in a Special Appeal: "SPECIAL APPEAL. ACTION FOR RECTIFICATION OF BIRTH REGISTRATION TO CHANGE NAME AND SEX (GENDER) FROM MALE TO FEMALE. TRANSSEXUAL PERSON. NO NEED FOR SEX REASSIGNMENT SURGERY. (1) In the light of the provisions of articles 55, 57 and 58 of Law 6.015/73 (Public Records Law), it can be inferred that the principle of immutability of the name, although of public order, can be mitigated when the individual interest or social benefit of the change stands out, which requires, in any case, duly motivated judicial authorisation, after a hearing with the Public Prosecutor's Office. (2) In the light of the provisions of Law 6.015/73 (Public Records Law), it can be inferred that the principle of immutability of the name, although of public order, can be mitigated when the individual interest or social benefit of the change stands out. From this perspective, subject to the need for intervention by the Judiciary, it is permissible to change a name that causes a vexatious situation or social degradation to the individual, such as those whose first names are notoriously classified as belonging to the male or female gender, but whose physical appearance and behavioural phenotype are completely at odds with the provisions of the registration act. (3) However, in the case of transsexuals, the mere change of name does not achieve the protective scope embodied in the infra-legal rule, as well as neglecting the imperative requirement of realising the constitutional principle of the dignity of the human person, which translates the anti-utilitarian maxim according to which each human being must be understood as an end in itself and not as a means to the realisation of other people's ends or collective goals. (4) This is because, if changing one's name means changing one's gender (from male to female or vice versa), maintaining the sex listed in the civil registry will preserve the incongruity between the data recorded and the person's gender identity, which will continue to be susceptible to all sorts of constraints in civil life, constituting a flagrant attack on the existential right inherent to the personality. (5) Thus, the legal certainty sought through the individualisation of the person in the eyes of the family and society - the *ratio essendi of* the public register, guided by the principles of publicity and truthfulness - must be reconciled with the fundamental principle of the dignity of the human person, which is the interpretative vector of the entire legal-constitutional order. (6) With this in mind, the STJ, when assessing cases of transsexuals who have undergone transgenitalisation surgery, has already allowed them to change their name and sex/gender in the civil registry (REsp 1.008.398/SP, Reporting Justice Nancy Andrighi, Third Panel, judged on 15.10.2009, DJe 18.11.2009; and REsp 737.993/MG, Reporting Justice João Otávio de Noronha, Fourth Panel, judged on 10.11.2009, DJe 18.12.2009). (7) The aforementioned case law should evolve to also cover non-operated transsexuals, thus giving maximum effectiveness to the constitutional principle of promoting the dignity of the human person, a general clause protecting the existential rights inherent in the personality, which today is conceived as a fundamental value of the legal system, implying the unavoidable duty to respect differences. 8 - This supreme value (and normative principle) involves a complex of fundamental rights and duties of all dimensions that protect the individual from any degrading or inhumane treatment, guaranteeing them minimum existential conditions for a dignified life and preserving their individuality and autonomy against any kind of state or third-party interference (vertical and horizontal effectiveness of fundamental rights). 9. From this perspective, the fundamental rights of non-operated transsexual people to identity (social treatment in accordance with their gender identity), to freedom of development and expression of the human personality (without undue state interference), to recognition before the law (regardless of whether medical procedures are carried out), to intimacy and privacy (protection of life choices), to equality and non-discrimination (elimination of factual inequalities that may place them in a situation of inferiority), to health (guarantee of biopsychophysical well-being) and to happiness (general well-being) must be safeguarded. (10) Consequently, in the light of the fundamental rights that are corollaries of the fundamental principle of human dignity, it can be inferred that the right of transsexuals to have their sex rectified in the civil registry cannot be conditioned on the requirement to undergo transgenitalisation surgery, which for many is unattainable from a financial point of view (as seems to be the case here) or even unfeasible from a medical point of view. (11) Furthermore, the so-called legal sex (that contained in the civil birth register, assigned in early childhood on the basis of the morphological, gonadic or chromosomal aspect) cannot overlook the psychosocial aspect arising from each individual's self-defined gender identity, which, in view of the *ratio essendi of* public registers, is the criterion that should, in this case, govern the individual's relations with society. 12) A contrary exegesis is incoherent in the face of the jurisprudential consecration of the right to rectify the registered sex conferred on transsexuals who have undergone surgery, who, nevertheless, continue to be bound to the biological/chromosomal sex that was repudiated. In other words, regardless of biological reality, the civil registry must portray the psychosocial gender identity of the transsexual person, who cannot be required to undergo

The legal protection of personality rights, as will be explained below, is of a constitutional, civil and criminal nature, based on the fundamental principle expressed in art. I°, III, of the Brazilian Constitution, that of the dignity of the human person. This principle, which guides and legitimises the legal system for the defence of personality, means that the human person is the foundation and end of society, the state and the law and, as such, pre-existent to them.

In this way, all rights, values, goods and interests related to the personality can (and should) be protected on the basis of the general clause protecting human dignity, even if there is no express normative provision.[20,21] So, as time goes by, new rights

What matters is the protection of everything that is important for the development and well-being of the person, in other words, the protection of their dignity. For example, today we talk about the environment as a personality right, a hybrid of psychophysical and moral integrity, which we didn't hear about with this meaning a few years ago. Likewise happiness, and there is even a proposal to include it as a fundamental right in art. 6° of the Constitution (PEC no. 19/2010).

The natural person is fundamentally made up of three aspects:
1. *Psychophysical:* refers to the person's physical body and their thoughts, made up of their limbs, organs, tissues and their psychological side. The personality rights that refer to this aspect have as their object the *psychophysical* or *psychosomatic integrity of* the person;
2. *Spiritual or moral:* this is not a religious definition of spirit. Here the meaning refers to feelings, sensitive inclinations, concepts that the person has of him/herself and that others have of that subject, in short, the person's immaterial situations. In this case, personality rights aim to ensure the *spiritual* or *moral integrity of* the person; and
3. *Intellectual:* refers to a person's ability to produce knowledge, invent and create. It therefore protects the creativity, intellectual production, invention and art that the individual produces and can produce. For this reason, personality rights deal with the *intellectual integrity of* the natural person.

Therefore, didactically, personality rights can be systematised as follows:

ASPECTS	CLASSIC RIGHTS	NEW RIGHTS
Psychosomatic (psychological and physical)	Life, physical integrity, health, integrity of organs and tissues, refusal of life-threatening medical treatment, freedom of movement, *etc.*	Psychological integrity, *anti-bullying, anti-mobbing,* healthy environment.
Spiritual or moral (feelings, convictions and intimacy)	Name, image, honour, privacy, modesty, peace and quiet, freedom of belief and religion, *etc.*	Equality for people with mental or physical disabilities, accessibility, working time, personal and sexual identity.
Intellectual (intelligence and creativity)	Freedom of expression, thought, information, copyright, intellectual property, industrial property, *etc.*	Anti-plagiarism actions and texts on social networks.

In this way, the personality rights known today constitute an exemplary or *numerus apertus* list and can be divided as follows:
1. *Rights to psychophysical integrity:* (biological) life, bodily integrity and the integrity of organs and tissues, prohibition of torture and psychological ill-treatment;
2. *Rights of moral integrity:* freedom, honour, fame, image, privacy, quiet, modesty; and

---

sex reassignment surgery in order to enjoy a right. 13 - Special appeal granted in order to uphold in full the initial claim, authorising the rectification of the plaintiff's civil registration, in which, in addition to the name indicated, the sex/gender of the female should be recorded, noting the existence of a court order, without mentioning the reason for or content of the changes made, safeguarding the publicity of the records and the privacy of the plaintiff" (STJ, REsp 1626739/RS, Rel. Minister LUIS FELIPE SALOMÃO, FOURTH COURT, judged on 09/05/2017).

3. *Intellectual integrity rights:* artistic and cultural production, authorship of music and books, paintings, trademarks, patents, inventions.

These rights may vary over time, as they refer to the current state of the art in the field.

This is what has happened with *accessibility, which* has been elevated to a fundamental right for people with locomotive disabilities. Because of its close relationship with human independence and freedom, accessibility can be considered a right of the personality.

CHAPTER 2

INJURIES TO PERSONALITY RIGHTS AND THEIR CONSEQUENCES

Personality rights are those inherent to the condition of being human, i.e. every person has them, regardless of social, political or economic status.

This is the protection of fundamental values, such as name, image, physical integrity, among others, which cannot be violated, under penalty of causing extra-patrimonial damage that can be remedied, in addition to the possibility of other remedies being applied by the courts.

2.1. Damage to personality.

Injury to personality rights has always been referred to as moral damage, so that every time someone's personality rights are disrespected, causing injury to their privacy, there is moral damage. Consequently, moral damage is an injury to human dignity[22] .

However, the *heading of* Article 12 of the Civil Code makes it clear that an injury to a personality right can also cause damage to property (losses and damages). For this reason, Fernando Noronha prefers to analyse the situation based on the damage suffered by the person[23] .

According to the author, it is convenient to distinguish between *damage, damaged property* and *damaged interest - property* is tangible or intangible things, as well as the internal qualities of people (biological, spiritual or affective); *interest* is the relationship between the person and the property, which can be economic or spiritual (affective); and *damage* is the harm caused to a property, which can be a thing, or the body or soul of a person[24 25 26] .

For Fernando Noronha, *damage is injury to a legal asset, with a reduction in its value.* This definition can then be analysed based on its fundamental elements[25,26] :

1. *Injury:* is the breach of a duty of safety, i.e. the integrity protected by law, of the legal asset;
2. *Legal property:* there are two types of property protected by the law, namely people and things. In this way, damage is characterised as a breach of a duty of safety or integrity of a person or thing;
3. *Reduction:* refers to the loss suffered when property is damaged. Such damage can be *off-balance sheet* (better known as *moral damage)* and/or *property* (better known as *property damage, material damage* or *loss and damage),* and
4. *Value:* in this case, Noronha follows the so-called values of the social world designated by Kant, which are price (things) and *dignity* (people), i.e. things have a price and people have dignity.

In this way, what is being protected is damage. Fernando Noronha's definition allows us to identify the existence of injuries associated with damage: damage to a person always entails off-balance sheet damage, and can also entail property damage; damage to a thing always entails property damage, and can also cause off-balance sheet damage. These consequences lead to an increase in the extent of the damage and the corresponding compensation (art. 944). Systematising:

DAMAGE/INJUR	LOSS	LEGAL BASIS

---

[22] MOARES, Maria Celina de. *Damage to the human person.* Rio de Janeiro: Renovar, 2003, p. 129-130.

[23] NORONHA, Fernando. *Law of obligations.* 4ª . ed. São Paulo: Saraiva, 2013, pp. 579 and ss.

[24] NORONHA, Fernando. *Law of obligations,* ob. cit., pp. 579-580.

[25] NORONHA, Fernando. *Direito das obrigações,* ob. cit., p. 579: damage is "the loss, economic or non-economic, of an individual or collective nature, which results from an unlawful act or fact that violates any value inherent to the human person, or affects something in the external world that is legally protected".

[26] SILVESTRE, Gilberto Fachetti. *Civil liability for breach of the social function of the contract.* São Paulo: Almedina, 2018, pp. 229-230.

Y		
To the person	Off balance sheet	Art. 12, *caput*, CC; art. 186, CC; art. 5º, V and X, CRFB.
To the person	Assets	Art. 12, *caput*, CC; art. 186, CC; art. 402, CC; art. 21, CC, art. 5º, V and X, CRFB.
The thing	Assets	Art. 186, CC; Art. 402, CC.
The thing	Off balance sheet	Art. 952, sole paragraph, CC.

We can see, therefore, that damage is not the violation of legal property, but the consequence of this violation. The violation of the property characterises an illicit act, i.e. an act contrary to the law, which may or may not result in damage[27].

Despite the various doctrinal classifications of damages, it is important to highlight the one that distinguishes them into *pecuniary damages* and *off-balance sheet damages* (commonly referred to as *moral damages)*, taking into account whether or not the damaged asset or interest is susceptible to economic evaluation. Based on what Fernando Noronha teaches, it can be said that pecuniary damage consists of the violation of goods and interests susceptible to pecuniary appreciation, while *off-balance* sheet *damage* consists of the offence against goods and interests that have no economic character[28].

Moral damage, from a general point of view, is intended to protect the rights of the personality, inherent to the condition of being human. This does not exclude the possibility of compensation for moral damage resulting from damage to property, which, in turn, also occurs, and there will be a combination of pecuniary and non-pecuniary damage.

Injuries to the personality are different in nature:

5. *Physical,* which is that which violates the bodily safety and mental health of the individual, typified in Chapters I to VI of Title I of the Special Part of the Penal Code; and
6. *Moral,* which affects - or can affect - the most intimate feelings of the human being, such as honour, well-being, and can cause bad sensations, such as suffering, pain, anguish, humiliation, etc.

The main difference is precisely the way in which this damage is perceived. In the case of physical damage, it is visible to anyone (anyone can, for example, visualise a mutilated limb, a wound or death). Moral damage, on the other hand, cannot often be visualised, as it affects a person's intimacy, their feelings, which are not visible and cannot be felt by other individuals. For this reason, this type of damage is independent of proof of suffering.

2.2. Characterisation of moral damage.

Property damage affects the set of goods and interests that make up the victim's assets and can be repaired by means of pecuniary compensation. In this case, the compensation must be sufficient to restore the victim to the situation prior to the unlawful act that caused the damage *(status quo ante)*. Under the terms of Article 402

---

[27] PONTES DE MIRANDA, Francisco Cavalcanti. *Treatise on Private Law.* Special Part. Volume LIII. Rights of Obligation. São Paulo: RT, 2012, p. 262; MARINONI, Luiz Guilherme. *Tort remedies:* Injunction and removal. Art. 497, sole paragraph, CPC/2015. São Paulo: Revista dos Tribunais, 2015, p. 24-28.

[28] NORONHA, Fernando. *Direito das obrigações,* ob. cit., pp. 590-594. You can see, therefore, that the origin of the damage (pecuniary or non-pecuniary) is the injury to the person or thing. This general situation is what constitutes damage. Two situations may well exemplify the damage that results from an injury to the personality: 1) Imagine the case in which a model is run over on a pedestrian crossing, is hospitalised, has her leg amputated and is unable to fulfil her contracts and practice her profession. The damage was to her physical integrity, in other words, to her person. Therefore, her dignity has been reduced and, consequently, there has been an off-balance sheet loss. But there is also a situation of pecuniary damage (loss and damage): the medical and hospital expenses; the loss of profit from the impossibility of fulfilling his contracts; and the loss of labour capacity; and 2) Another example is the visually impaired person who depends on a guide dog to get around. Of course, in this case the relationship between the owner and the thing is different, and there is also an emotional relationship between them. For this reason, if someone runs over and kills this dog, the damage will be greater than the losses and damages (the price of the animal), but it will also affect the personality of the visually impaired person: it takes away the thing that allows them to exercise their freedom, despite their visual limitation, and deprives them of a thing with which they have an intimate and differentiated relationship of affection, thus constituting damage to their dignity (off balance sheet).

of the Civil Code, property damage can be categorised as:

1. *Emergent damage:* in the words of Sérgio Cavalieri Filho, it consists of "the effective and immediate reduction of the victim's assets"[29] ; and

2. *Loss of profit:* the loss of the expected gain, i.e. the increase in assets that would have occurred if the damage had not occurred.

On the other hand, off-balance sheet damage cannot be fully compensated by monetary compensation alone, since, as a rule, the goods and interests that have been damaged are not subject to economic evaluation[30] .

However, although the attributes of the human person are not subject to pecuniary assessment, the violation of an individual's rights to physical, psychological, moral and intellectual integrity can give rise to pecuniary and non-pecuniary damage. For example, defamation of a liberal professional can simultaneously cause: a reduction in his clientele and, consequently, a reduction in profits (property damage); and an offence to his subjective honour, understood as a personal feeling of esteem (off-balance sheet damage). Another example: paraplegia, as well as causing a reduction in labour capacity and therefore property damage, also causes psychological suffering and offence to the victim's aesthetics (off-balance sheet damage)[31] .

In any case, according to Anderson Schreiber, "injury to any of the rights of the personality, whether expressly recognised by the Civil Code or not, constitutes moral damage"[32] , i.e. off-balance sheet damage.

Moral damage can therefore be defined as an *injury to a property, attribute or value of the personality.* Therefore, whenever there is an offence against a personality right, there will be, *in re ipsa*, an off-balance sheet loss, which may also be associated with a property loss. In other words, every transgression of a personality right will inevitably result in moral damage, which may, depending on the circumstances, be associated with other damage, this one of a patrimonial nature. In short: the violation of personality rights will always cause non-pecuniary damage and, eventually, pecuniary damage[33] .

For off-balance sheet damage to be characterised, proof of pain, suffering, vexation, humiliation, sadness *etc.* is not required.

In Brazilian legal history, the understanding of moral damage can be divided into three historical-legal-doctrinal moments:

3. *From the Civil Code of 1916 to the Constitution of the Republic of 1988:* compensation for moral damage was not allowed, as the Civil Code only regulated compensation for property damage. The rationale was that compensation for a non-economic value could not be expressed in monetary terms;

4. *From the Constitution of the Republic of 1988 to the Civil Code of 2002:* items V and X of art. 5º CRFB admit compensation for moral damage. Although the damage is irreparable and has no corresponding economic value, it is allowed to be compensated in monetary terms as an indemnity for the offence caused. At this point, moral damage is associated with the subjective honour (sense of self) and suffering of the victim, in other words, this off-balance sheet damage should cause pain to the victim, which is precisely why moral damage is referred to as the price of pain *(pretium doloris).*

---

[29] CAVALIERI FILHO, Sérgio. *Civil liability programme.* 1 Iª ed. São Paulo: Atlas, 2014, p. 94.

[30] KANT, Immanuel. The metaphysics of morals. São Paulo: Martin Claret, 2002, pp. 33-34, explains that things have a price and people have dignity. These are the socially accepted values that are affected when a duty of safety is violated. Such damage causes a reduction in these values: "In the realm of ends, everything has either a price or a dignity. When a thing has a price, any other thing can be put in its place as an equivalent, but when a thing is above all price, and therefore allows no equivalent, then it has dignity [...]. This judgement therefore recognises the value of such a disposition of mind as dignity and places it infinitely above any price. It could never be put into calculation or comparison with anything that had a price, without in any way harming its sanctity?"

[31] NORONHA, Fernando. *Law of obligations,* ob. cit., p. 592.

[32] SCHREIBER, Anderson. *Personality rights.* 3ª ed. São Paulo: Atlas, 2014, p. 16.

[33] SILVESTRE, Gilberto Fachetti; HIBNER, Davi Amaral. The protection of personality rights in Brazil and Italy: material and procedural issues. In: *II International Civil Procedure Congress,* 2017, Vitória. Proceedings of the 2nd International Civil Procedure Congress. Vitória: UFES, 2017. v. 1. pp. 11-26; HIBNER, Davi Amaral. *The protection of personality rights in the 2015 Code of Civil Procedure.* Master's dissertation. Postgraduate Programme in Law. Federal University of Espírito Santo. Supervisor: Prof Dr Gilberto Fachetti Silvestre. Vitória, 2018-2019, Chap. 1.

The problem is proving this suffering, which is true diabolical proof *(probatio diabólica* or *devil's sproofy,* e

5. *From the Civil Code of 2002 onwards:* moral damage is independent of suffering and injury to the victim's subjective honour. Moral damage arises from an objective injury to personality rights, i.e. the violation of a duty of safety, regardless of the victim's suffering or feelings. Thus, the damage is associated with the victim's objective honour (the notion that people have) and we speak of damage *in re ipsa,* i.e. *ipso jure.*

Therefore, in the event of a violation of personality rights, off-balance sheet damage will be established by the simple offence against highly personal legal assets, regardless of the negative (and subjective) feelings generated within the victim[34] . Thus, in the event of an offence against personality rights, off-balance sheet damage occurs *in re ipsa* or *ipso facto.* For example, the improper use of a person's image, even if it is not for commercial or economic purposes, causes off-balance sheet damage, and it is unnecessary to demonstrate damage in order to be compensated.

In order to constitute moral damage, it is also necessary for the injury to be serious, going beyond the normal patterns of everyday life. Daily annoyance resulting from the human relationships inherent to life in society is not capable of giving rise to compensation for moral damage. In this respect, Sérgio Cavalieri Filho says[35] :

> [...] only pain, vexation, suffering or humiliation that, beyond normality, intensely interferes with the psychological behaviour of the individual, causing them distress, anguish and imbalance in their well-being, should be considered moral damage. Mere dissatisfaction, annoyance, hurt, irritation or exacerbated sensitivity are outside the orbit of moral damage, because, in addition to being part of the normality of our daily lives, at work, in traffic, among friends and even in the family environment, such situations are not intense and long-lasting, to the point of breaking the individual's psychological balance. If this is not understood, we will end up trivialising moral damage, giving rise to lawsuits seeking compensation for the most trivial annoyances.

The mere discomfort of everyday life is not capable of giving rise to compensation for moral damage and does not give rise to pecuniary satisfaction.

On this point, it should be noted that although Sérgio Cavalieri Filho talks about pain, embarrassment or suffering, the author emphasises that these feelings are not causes of moral damage, i.e. they cannot be considered requirements for moral damage to be established, but are consequences that may or may not occur when there is a violation of an individual's human dignity: "From this perspective, moral damage is not necessarily linked to some psychic reaction of the victim. There can be an offence against the dignity of the human person without pain, embarrassment or suffering, just as there can be pain, embarrassment and suffering without a violation of dignity. Pain, embarrassment and suffering can be consequences and not causes"[36] .

Therefore, what is meant by mere dissatisfaction that is not capable of constituting moral damage are everyday situations, the common wear and tear of everyday life or mere annoyance.

The establishment of moral damage does not require proof of psychological reactions. However, it is necessary for the violation of the right to be so serious as to give rise to pecuniary compensation, for example, when the violation of rights causes the curtailment of the individual's freedom, which occurs when the right to accessibility is not respected.

2.3. Judicial protection of personality rights.

There are two ways of protecting personality rights:

1. *Self-defence:* when the holder of the right can take measures to prevent the damage from occurring or continuing to occur, in the imminence of the agent's action or during that damaging action. E.g.

---

[34] MORAES, Maria Celina de. *Damage to the human person.* Rio de Janeiro: Renovar, 2003, p. 131.

[35] CAVALIERI FILHO, Sérgio. *Civil liability programme.* 1 Iª ed. São Paulo: Atlas, 2014, p. 111.

[36] CAVALIERI FILHO, Sérgio. *Civil liability programme,* ob. cit.

legitimate defence (art. 188 of the Civil Code); and

2. *Heterotutelage:* refers to cases in which the damage has already occurred or is likely to occur, as well as, of course, when the victim is unable to practise self-tutelage. To this end, the individual will turn to the state for help, which is why it is also called state protection, which can be exercised in two ways:
   - *by administrative means:* when the individual appeals to the police authority; and
   - *by judicial means:* when the individual resorts to the judiciary through actions for damages, compensation, obligations to do or not to do.

According to José dos Santos Bedaque, judicial protection "is the set of measures established by the procedural legislator in order to give effectiveness to a life situation protected by substantial law"[37].

Along the same lines, Luiz Guilherme Marinoni states that "protection is not just the judgement, but the set of means available to procedural law to adequately meet the provisions of substantial law", in other words, "the set of measures suitable for protecting the good of life sought by the court in the process"[38].

In Brazil, the procedural protection of personality rights takes the form of four types of protection[39]:

1. *Injunctions,* including *injunctions',*
2. *Reintegration* or *removal of the offence',*
3. *Restorative* (or *compensation in the specific form)',* and
4. *Compensatory* damages, covering both *compensation* for moral damage and *compensation* for property damage.

By the way, Cristiano Chaves de Farias and Nelson Rosenvald summarise the protection of personality rights as follows[40]:

> [...] Article 12 of the Substantive Law states that the legal protection of personality rights, in civil law (without prejudice to criminal protection), will take the form of repressive measures - the so-called classic protection of personality - and, likewise, preventive measures - the so-called specific protection (which can be individual or collective, regulated, respectively, by Articles 497 of the Code of Civil Procedure and 84 of the Consumer Defence Code). [...] In other words, in addition to preventive and compensatory protection of personality rights, there is also the possibility of reintegrative protection, in the specific form, the aim of which is to naturally restore the situation prior to the unlawful act that has already taken place, without the offended party needing to use the mechanism of reparation.

Along the same lines, Elimar Szaniawski writes[41]:

> In addition to self-defence of the personality, which we all have, Article 12 of the Civil Code comprehensively protects personality rights, providing the necessary means for anyone who is about to suffer an attack on a personality right to stop the threat or injury and claim damages.

Injunctive relief, including *injunctive relief,* consists of a set of measures designed to prevent the offence from occurring and/or to prevent its continuation and/or reiteration. Better

clarifying, injunctive relief serves to prevent the *commission of the offence,* the *repetition of the offence* and *the continuation of the offence*2*.

---

[37] BEDAQUE, José Roberto dos Santos. *Law and Process.* Influence of material law on process. 6ª ed. São Paulo: Malheiros, 2006, p. 36.

[38] MARINONI, Luiz Guilherme. *Tort remedies: injunctions and injunctive relief.* Art. 497, sole paragraph, CPC/2015. São Paulo: Revista dos Tribunais, 2015, pp. 214-215.

[39] SILVESTRE, Gilberto Fachetti; HIBNER, Davi Amaral. The protection of personality rights in Brazil and Italy: material and procedural issues, ob. cit. *The protection of personality rights in the 2015 Code of Civil Procedure,* ob. cit.

[40] FARIAS, Cristiano Chaves de; ROSENVALD, Nelson. *Civil Law Course.* General Part and LINDB. Vol. 1. 15ª ed. Salvador: JusPodivm, 2017, pp. 212-214.

[41] SZANIAWSKI, Elimar. *Direitos de personalidade e sua tutela.* 2ª ed. São Paulo: Revista dos Tribunais, 2005, p. 248.

Its aim is to prevent the violation of the substantive right, preventing the unlawful act from taking place. It is, therefore, protection against a threat to the right, in other words, protection against a future offence, "even if this is configured as a repetition or continuation of a previous offence", according to Luiz Guilherme Marinoni[42][43].

In the Brazilian legal system, injunctive relief, including cessation, is provided for in the *head* paragraph *of* Article 12 of the Civil Code and the sole paragraph of Article 497 of the Code of Civil Procedure, which are applicable to the protection of personality rights, with the aim of preventing or stopping unlawful acts that harm the physical, psychic-moral, spiritual and intellectual integrity of the human person[44].

Although injunctive relief is covered by injunctive relief (under the terms of the sole paragraph of art. 497 of the CPC), they should be differentiated for didactic purposes only. While injunctive relief is intended to prevent the offence from being committed, injunctive relief serves to prevent its continuation or reiteration. The purpose of injunctive relief, therefore, is to put an end to unlawful acts with ongoing effects, while injunctive relief is designed to prevent unlawful acts that have never occurred[45].

Thus, injunctive relief comprises a set of measures designed to extirpate the continuation of an offence that is prolonged over time, i.e. that does not disappear in just one act or that is perpetuated over time. This is the case, for example, with systematic intimidation, better known as *bullying* (Law no. 13.185/2015).

As a rule, injunctive relief will be combined with compensatory/indemnity relief, since it will be necessary to repair any damage caused by the unlawful act.

As an example of injunctive relief, we can mention the protective measures provided for in the Maria da Penha Law (articles 18 to 23 of Law No. 11.340/2006), which aim to protect the woman's physical and psychological-moral integrity, with the purpose of preventing the offence and/or preventing its continuation or reiteration.

Furthermore, based on Article 105 of Law No. 9,610/1998, it is possible to grant injunctive relief for the suspension or interruption of the transmission or retransmission of musical works in the programme of a company that is in default with the prior payment of copyright to ECAD (Central Office for Collection and Distribution).

Injunctive relief, therefore, is designed to prevent the offence from occurring and/or to prevent its continuation or reiteration.

In the Brazilian legal system, *injunctive* relief (or removal of the wrongful act) is regulated in the final part of the sole paragraph of art. 497 of the Code of Civil Procedure, which aims to remove or eliminate the effects of the wrongful act carried out[46]. In this sense, Davi Amaral Hibner explains[47]: "The remedy of removal of the unlawful act or reintegration, regulated in the final part of the sole paragraph of art. 497 of the CPC/2015, aims to remove or eliminate the effects of the unlawful act practised, in order to re-establish the situation that existed prior to the violation of the right."

It is, therefore, "jurisdictional protection aimed at enforcing the desire of the violated rule, that is, it is protection to remove the effects that would be present in reality were it not for the violation of the rule", in the words of Luiz Guilherme Marinoni[48]. In the same vein, Bruno Marzullo Zaroni and Paula Pessoa Pereira argue that "injunctive relief is not intended to prevent the continuation or repetition of the offence (the aim of

---

[42] SILVESTRE, Gilberto Fachetti; HIBNER, Davi Amaral. The protection of personality rights in Brazil and Italy: material and procedural issues, ob. cit.

[43] MARINONI, Luiz Guilherme. *Injunctions and remedies against unlawful acts,* ob. cit.

[44] SILVESTRE, Gilberto Fachetti; HIBNER, Davi Amaral. The protection of personality rights in Brazil and Italy: material and procedural issues, ob. cit.

[45] SILVESTRE, Gilberto Fachetti; HIBNER, Davi Amaral. The protection of personality rights in Brazil and Italy: material and procedural issues, ob. cit.

[46] SILVESTRE, Gilberto Fachetti; HIBNER, Davi Amaral. The protection of personality rights in Brazil and Italy: material and procedural issues, ob. cit.

[47] HIBNER, Davi Amaral. *The protection of personality rights in the 2015 Code of Civil Procedure,* ob. cit.

[48] MARINONI, Luiz Guilherme. *Injunctions and remedies against unlawful acts,* ob. cit.

injunctions). Its foundation is the illicit act of continued effectiveness"[49] .

An example of reinstatement is the "injunction granted to remove the image of a person who has been unduly included in a commercial advertisement on the internet".[50]

There are differences between injunctions and reintegration injunctions. While injunctive relief is designed to prevent the commission, repetition or continuation of an offence, restorative relief is aimed at the effects of the offence that has already been committed[51] .

Thus, based on the fundamental rights to effectiveness and to a procedural technique that is adequate to protect the material right (arts. 4º and 6º of the CPC), injunctive relief and reinstatement relief must be understood, respectively, as remedies capable of: preventing the unlawful act or inhibiting its reiteration or continuation, and eliminating its concrete effects, as Luiz Guilherme Marinoni states[52] .

According to Fredie Didier Jr, Leonardo Carneiro da Cunha, Paula Samo Braga and Rafael Alexandria de Oliveira, "there is nothing to prevent the remedy from being both reintegratory and inhibitory: a continuing offence or its effects are removed and a new offence or the continuation of the offence removed is prevented"[53] .

In turn, *restorative protection* (or compensation in the specific form) is aimed at repairing the damage. Reparation means "returning to the previous appearance" *(re + paribus)*. It's a return to the *status quo ante,* which is why we talk about restoring personality[54] .

This is a form of protection "capable of restoring the violated legal good, with reparation for the damage by non-pecuniary means, with the aim of re-establishing the state prior to the injury"[55] .

Examples of restorative protection include: the right of reply - provided for in article 5º , V, of the CRFB - or the right of the offended party to rectify a story published or broadcast by a media outlet, which must be exercised in accordance with Law 13.188/15; and public or private retraction.

The Superior Court of Justice admits reinstatement as a means of repairing damage to personal rights, by granting the right of reply[56] :

> The right to reply, to clarify the truth, to rectify false information or to retract, based on the Constitution and Civil Law, has not been ruled out; on the contrary, it was expressly recognised by the Supreme Court's ruling in ADPF 130. This is specific protection, based on the principle of full reparation, in order to preserve the purpose and effectiveness of the institute of civil liability (Civil Code, arts. 927 and 944).

In the Italian legal system, restorative relief is also provided for in article 2.058, paragraph 1, of the Civil Code, according to which: "The injured party may request reinstatement in a specific form, if it is totally or partially possible."

The purpose of compensation is to redress or compensate for the damage caused by an act that offends

[49] ZARONI, Bruno Marzullo; PEREIRA, Paula Pessoa. Injunctive relief in the new CPC. In: DIDIER JR. Fredie; MACEDO, Lucas Buril de; PEIXOTO, Ravi; and FREIRE, Alexandre (Org.). *New CPC. Selected Doctrine. Execution.* Vol. 5. 2ª ed. Salvador: JusPodivm, 2017, p. 254.

[50] HIBNER, Davi Amaral. *The protection of personality rights in the 2015 Code of Civil Procedure,* ob. cit.

[51] MARINONI, Luiz Guilherme. *Procedural technique and protection of rights.* 5ª ed. São Paulo: Brasil, 2018, p. 188; SILVESTRE, Gilberto Fachetti; HIBNER, Davi Amaral. The protection of personality rights in Brazil and Italy: material and procedural issues, ob. cit.

[52] MARINONI, Luiz Guilherme. *Tutela contra o ilícito: inibitória e de remoção,* ob. cit.

[53] DIDIER JR., Fredie; CUNHA, Leonardo Carneiro da; BRAGA, Paula Samo; OLIVEIRA, Rafael Alexandria de. *Civil Procedural Law Course. Execution.* Vol. 5. 7ª ed. Salvador: JusPodivm, 2017, p. 575.

[54] SILVESTRE, Gilberto Fachetti; HIBNER, Davi Amaral. The protection of personality rights in Brazil and Italy: material and procedural issues, ob. cit. *The protection of personality rights in the 2015 Code of Civil Procedure,* ob. cit.

[55] HIBNER, Davi Amaral. *The protection of personality rights in the 2015 Code of Civil Procedure,* ob. cit.

[56] STJ, REsp. nº. 1.440.721/GO, 4ª Turma, Rei. Min. Maria Isabel Gallotti, j. on 11/10/2016.

personality rights. It includes: *compensation,* which aims to redress pecuniary damage (emergent damage and loss of profits), so that the victim can return to the *status quo ante,* with the payment of a monetary sum corresponding to the damage; and *compensation, which* consists of the payment of a pecuniary sum to *compensate* for the off-balance sheet damage[57].

By way of systematisation, the jurisdictional protection of personality rights in Brazil can be summarised as follows[58]:

TUTELA	OBJECT
Compensation	This is a type of compensatory and repressive remedy which, as a rule, presupposes the occurrence of an offence and damage. It consists of the payment of a pecuniary sum, the aim of which is to compensate for the patrimonial damage felt by the holder of an injured personality right. Its value is obtained through a mathematical operation of subtraction, which corresponds to the difference between the assets that existed before the harmful event and the assets reduced after the injury. It is a question of removing the damage *(in* = no; *denne* = damage). In this case, there is the possibility of the victim returning to the *status quo ante.* Although self-defence is lawful conduct, it can cause damage for which the perpetrator must be held responsible (articles 188 and 929, both of the Civil Code), which is why the granting of compensation does not always depend on the occurrence of an unlawful act.
Compensatory	This is a type of compensatory and repressive remedy. It consists of the payment of a pecuniary sum to compensate for off-balance sheet damage. This amount is arrived at through judicial arbitration.
Inhibitory	This is preventive relief, consisting of the application of measures aimed at preventing the occurrence, repetition or continuation of the offence. It is granted regardless of the occurrence of damage and proof of fault (sole paragraph of art. 497 of the CPC). Its effectiveness depends essentially on the setting of *astreintes* (arts. 536, §1, and 537 of the CPC).
Termination	This is a type (or species) of injunctive relief. It consists of a set of measures aimed at preventing the *reiteration* or *continuation of* the offence. It is applied in cases where
	the injury (the tort) is prolonged over time, i.e. it doesn't disappear in just one act. It is repeated frequently and/or perpetuated over time. As a rule, this protection will be associated with indemnity/compensation, since it will be necessary to repair the damage caused by the offence.
Reintegration (to remove the offence)	This is repressive protection. It consists of a set of measures aimed at removing the effects of the offence committed, seeking the reintegration or reconstitution of the violated right. As is the case with injunctions and injunctions for damages, the granting of injunctions is independent of the demonstration of damage and the existence of guilt (sole paragraph of art. 497 of the CPC).
Restorative (specific form of compensation)	Repressive protection, provided after the offence and damage. It is aimed at restoring the violated legal asset, with reparation of damages by non-pecuniary means, so that the *status quo ante is* restored. It is granted after the offence and damage have been committed. Reparation means "to return to the previous appearance" (re + *paribus).*

The Brazilian legal system, therefore, has mechanisms capable of broadly protecting personality rights, making it possible to prevent unlawful behaviour and to repair and compensate for damage resulting from injury to the fundamental attributes of the human person.

---

[57] SILVESTRE, Gilberto Fachetti; HIBNER, Davi Amaral. The protection of personality rights in Brazil and Italy: material and procedural issues, ob. cit.

[58] HIBNER, Davi Amaral. *As tutelas dos direitos da personalidade no Código de Processo Civil de 2015,* ob. cit., Chap. 3; and SILVESTRE, Gilberto Fachetti; HIBNER, Davi Amaral. The protection of personality rights in Brazil and Italy: material and procedural issues, ob. cit.

CHAPTER 3

THE CONVENTION ON THE RIGHTS OF PERSONS WITH DISABILITIES

Between 2002 and 2006, the United Nations Organisation, through an *Ad Hoc* Committee *of the General Assembly,* negotiated the creation of the Convention on the Rights of Persons with Disabilities and its Optional Protocol.

Eight sessions were held until, on 13 December 2006, the Convention and its Protocol were adopted at the United Nations headquarters in New York. This is considered to be the fastest negotiation of a human rights treaty.

The following year, on 30 March 2007, the documents were opened for signature, reaching 82 signatures for the Convention, 44 for the Optional Protocol and 1 ratification on the first day.

A historical analysis shows that the number of signatures was the highest on the first day of a United Nations Convention[59] , which demonstrates the great importance and worldwide interest in further regulating the rights of people with disabilities.

Brazil was one of the signatories of the Convention and its Optional Protocol on the first day, but ratification only took place on 9 July 2008, passing through the approval quorum provided for in § 3° , of art. 5° , of the Constitution of the Republic, according to which international treaties and conventions on human rights that are approved in each house of Congress, in two rounds, by three-fifths of the votes of the respective members, will be equivalent to Constitutional Amendments.

The Convention and its Protocol are instruments that seek to ensure that people with disabilities have their fundamental rights and individual freedoms respected, and are clearly an instrument for protecting human rights.

Thus, when it was approved with a special quorum, the Convention gained constitutional force in the Brazilian legal system, and came into force domestically in 2009, with Decree No. 6,949 of 25 August 2009.

The Convention on the Rights of Persons with Disabilities consists of a Preamble and 50 articles, and its Optional Protocol consists of a further 18 articles.

In this regard, Heloisa Helena Barboza and Vitor de Azevedo Almeida Júnior list three highlights of the Convention:[60]

> To begin with, three things should be emphasised about the Convention: a) its drafting involved significant participation by civil society, notably Non-Governmental Organisations (NGOs), and representations of people with disabilities; b) its purpose is to protect and ensure the full and equal enjoyment of all human rights and fundamental freedoms by all people with disabilities and to promote respect for their inherent dignity, thus placing the issue of disability on the human rights agenda; c) the frank adoption of the "social model" of disability, which completely and profoundly changes the understanding and legislative treatment of the matter.

It is worth presenting a general analysis for a better understanding of the changes brought about by this Convention, now considered a milestone in the history of the Rights of Persons with Disabilities.

3.1. Objectives of the Convention.

The treatment of people with disabilities has not always been aimed at protecting them. On the contrary, in the early days of civilisation, such people were treated as strange, abnormal beings. In ancient Greece, for example, there were laws that allowed for the elimination or segregation of people with disabilities. In Rome, too, the

---

[59] https://www.un.org/development/desa/disabilities/convention-on-the-rights-of-persons-with-disabilities.html
[60] BARBOZA, Heloisa Helena; ALMEIDA JÚNIOR, Vitor de Azevedo. Recognition and inclusion of people with disabilities. *Brazilian Journal of Civil Law.* Belo Horizonte, vol. 13, p. 17-37,2017.

law allowed for the elimination of children with apparent deformities[61] . This practice of eliminating and segregating people with disabilities lasted for many centuries, passing through the Middle Ages and the Modern Age without much change. The lack of any respect can even be seen in the nomenclatures used to describe them, calling them "deformed" or "monstrous".

With the emergence of the French Revolution's ideals of liberty, equality, fraternity and solidarity, people with disabilities began to have a place in social discussions, so that attempts were made to include them and recognise their fundamental rights. However, this process has not been quick and has continued to the present day, although it cannot be said that it has been consolidated[62] .

In the 20th century, especially after the Second World War, the concern with inclusion began to grow, because the great wars left behind many survivors with physical and mental sequelae, thus creating the need to rehabilitate them[63] .

The changes were gradual. At first, the International Labour Organisation (ILO) was created, which sought, among other things, to improve working conditions for people with disabilities. Later, in 1975, the Declaration of the Rights of Persons with Disabilities was signed by UN Resolution 2,542, a document that seeks to ensure that the implementation of public and economic policies takes into account the possible disabilities of human beings[64] . In 1982, the UN approved the World Programme of Action for People with Disabilities.

It can be said that it was from then on that a more significant transformation took place in the consolidation of the rights of these people. This programme established a series of measures to promote rehabilitation in order to include people with disabilities in society with full participation, in order to overcome the physical and social barriers imposed on them[65] .

Initially, it is clear from reading the Preamble that the main assumptions of the Convention are human rights and their accessibility to all people, in order to guarantee that people with disabilities can also have all their rights and freedoms respected, as well as having the principles of the United Nations Charter, the World Programme of Action for Disabled People and the Standards on the Equalisation of Opportunities for Persons with Disabilities put into practice.

There is also recognition of the different forms of disability and, above all, a significant change in its concept, which is now considered to be the result of the interaction between people and the barriers that prevent them from fully and effectively participating in society on an equal footing with others.

Finally, there is a clear intention to guarantee the autonomy and freedom of people with disabilities, so that they can make their own choices when interacting with themselves and their social relationships.

Heloisa Helena Barboza and Vitor de Azevedo Almeida Júnior point out that point "e" of the Preamble to the Convention established a new *social model* for the inclusion of people with disabilities, with the main effect being "the inversion of the perspective in the appreciation of disability, which is no longer a unilateral issue, of the individual, but is thought of, developed and worked on as a bilateral relationship, in which society effectively becomes the protagonist, with legal duties to fulfil"[66] .

In the same vein, Aline de Miranda Valverde Terra and Ana Carolina Brochado Teixeira emphasise the

---

[61] JAQUES, Karina. Fundamental right to accessibility. Online. Accessed on: 19 Apr. 2017.

[62] JAQUES, Karina. Fundamental right to accessibility, ob. cit. Accessed on: 19 Apr. 2017.

[63] NISHIYAMA, Adolfo Mamoru; TEIXEIRA, Carla Noura. The historical evolution of the protection of people with disabilities in Brazilian constitutions: current normative instruments for their realisation. In: *Revista de Direito Privado*, Vol. 68/2016, Aug/2016, pp. 225-240.

[64] JAQUES, Karina. Fundamental right to accessibility, ob. cit. Accessed on: 19 Apr. 2017.

[65] PEREIRA, R. V.; LELIS, H. R. Equality and Human Dignity of People with Disabilities: Reflections of the New Inclusion Law - Law no. 13.146/2015 - in the Health Sector. In: *Revista Brasileira de Direitos e Garantias Fundamentais*, 2(1), 2016, pp. 19-35.

[66] BARBOZA, Heloisa Helena; ALMEIDA JÚNIOR, Vitor de Azevedo. Recognition and inclusion of people with disabilities. *Brazilian Journal of Civil Law*. Belo Horizonte, vol. 13, p. 17-37,2017.

paradigm shift brought about by the assumption in paragraph "e" of the Convention's preamble[67] :

> A decisive contribution to this paradigm shift in Brazilian law was the adoption, alongside the medical model of disability - a model adopted exclusively by the Civil Code of 1916 and by the original wording of the Civil Code of 2002, which considered only the physical pathology (and the associated symptom) that gave rise to a disability - of the social model, introduced by the International Classification of Functioning, Disability and Health, published by the World Health Organisation in 2001, according to which the issue of disability is mainly a problem created by society.

It is on the basis of these and the other assumptions contained in the Preamble that the states parties to the Convention drafted the other articles.

Article I° sets out the purpose and one of the most important concepts to understand before starting to study accessibility, namely that of a person with a disability.

The purpose can be extracted from all the above and consists of "promoting, protecting and ensuring the full and equal enjoyment of all human rights and fundamental freedoms by all persons with disabilities and promoting respect for their inherent dignity".

As for the new concept of person with a disability, so does Article I° of the UN Convention:

> [...] are those who have long-term physical, mental, intellectual or sensory impairments which, in interaction with various barriers, may obstruct their full and effective participation in society on equal terms with others.

This concept goes beyond the limits of personal conditions and is determined on the basis of the worsening of natural limitations due to social barriers, i.e. it is a relational concept, in which disability arises from the interaction of a person's specific attributes with the barriers of the environment, hindering their full participation in society[68] .

As stated in the Preamble to the Convention, the concept of a person with a disability is constantly evolving, which can be seen from the nomenclatures used over the years.

Disabled, exceptional, handicapped - all these terms were used over the years, until the Convention brought a new terminology with a new meaning, which goes beyond a merely theoretical analysis, directly affecting the way in which people with disabilities are viewed by legislation, as well as by society.

The new concept gives people with disabilities greater autonomy and freedom, since their participation in society is not limited by personal characteristics, but rather by environmental barriers, which must be eliminated, since what is sought, in general, is the full and effective participation of these people in society on equal terms with others. It is, therefore, a definition more focused on social autonomy than on the medical and biological view, as Mateus de Oliveira Fomasier and Flavia Piva Almeida Leite point out[69] :

---

[67] TERRA, Aline de Miranda Valverde; TEIXEIRA, Ana Carolina Brochado. Reflections from the 1st International Encounter on the Rights of Persons with Disabilities in the Private Law of Spain, Brazil, Italy and Portugal. *Brazilian Journal of Civil Law*. Belo Horizonte, vol. 15, p. 223-233, Jan./Mar. 2018.

[68] FERRAZ, Carolina Valença; LEITE, Glauber Salomão. Brazilian inclusion law and the "new" concept of disability: will it "catch on" now? Available at: <http://justificando.cartacapital.com.br/2015/08/20/lei- brasileira-de-inclusao-e-o-novo-conceito-de-de-deficiencia-sera-que-agora-vai-pegar/>. Accessed on: 13 June 2017.

[69] FORNASIER, Mateus de Oliveira; LEITE, Flavia Piva Almeida. Fundamental rights to accessibility and urban mobility for people with disabilities: a systemic-autopoietic approach. In: *Revista de Direito da Cidade,* vol. 08, n° 3, 2016, p. 929. Similarly, MENEZES, Joyceane Bezerra de. Protective law in Brazil after the convention on the protection of persons with disabilities: impacts of the new CPC and the statute of persons with disabilities. In: *Civilistica.com.* Rio de Janeiro, a. 4, n. 1, jan.-jun.Jun./2015, p. 5, emphasises that the ratio of the Convention on the Rights of Persons with Disabilities revolves around participation, equality and autonomy, so much so that the concept of disability is no longer

[...] the main contribution of this Convention was to change the view of disability from the medical model to the social model of human rights, in which disability is the result of an equation that has two variables, namely the functional limitations of the human body and the numerous barriers imposed on the individual by society and the environment. Thus, the new paradigm of disability based on human rights is the vision or social model, according to which the environment has a direct influence on the freedom of the person with functional limitations, who may have their situation worsened because of their surroundings and not because of their characteristics per se.

The following articles seek to reinforce the purpose of the Convention, establishing general principles and obligations to be fulfilled by the signatory states. To this end, the states parties are obliged to adopt all legislative and administrative measures, raising public awareness of the needs of people with disabilities and abolishing any stereotypes and prejudice towards them.

It also emphasises that the Convention cannot be used as a pretext to reduce rights provided for in the domestic legislation of each state party, since the Convention will not affect any of these provisions, but is intended to broaden access to these rights.

The Convention also emphasises the special protection of children and women and girls, as they are subject to multiple forms of discrimination, and stresses the obligation of states parties to guarantee and promote the full exercise of fundamental rights on an equal basis with others, taking into account the best interests of the child.

There are also provisions specifically aimed at the autonomy and freedom of people with disabilities, especially with regard to respect for home and family, guaranteeing their freedom to start a family, marry, adopt and maintain their fertility, rights that could previously be restricted due to the concepts of incapacity provided for in domestic legislation.

By way of example, in Brazil, the marriage of a "mentally ill person" without the necessary discernment for the acts of civil life was null and void, according to Article 1.548,1 of the Civil Code, repealed by Law No. 13.146/2015.

3.2. Personal mobility in the Convention.

Moving on to the subject of accessibility, it is worth highlighting the provisions on personal mobility, independent living and inclusion in the community and access to work and employment, since in order for all these rights to be guaranteed, accessibility is necessary, i.e. "access, on an equal basis with others, to the physical environment, to transport, to information and communication, including information and communication systems and technologies, and to other services and facilities open to the public or for public use, in both urban and rural areas" (Article 9, 1, of the Convention on the Rights of Persons with Disabilities).

Under Article 9(1)(a) and (b) of the Convention, measures to ensure accessibility must be applied to: *(i)* buildings, roads, means of transport and other indoor and outdoor facilities, including schools, homes, medical facilities and the workplace; and *(ii)* information, communications and other services, including electronic services and emergency services.

For its part, Article 9(2) of the Convention lays down various obligations for States Parties to ensure full accessibility for people with disabilities. 9 of the Convention lays down a number of duties for States Parties in order to guarantee full accessibility for people with disabilities: *(i)* develop, promulgate and monitor the implementation of minimum standards and guidelines for the accessibility of facilities and services open to the public or for public use; *(ii)* ensure that private entities offering facilities and services open to the public or for public use take into account all aspects relating to accessibility for persons with disabilities; *(ii)* provide

---

biopsychological, but rather the difficulty of overcoming barriers of all kinds: "The CRPD abandons the understanding of disability as an intrinsic aspect of the person, to understand it as a lasting limitation that is aggravated by the interaction of natural impediments with social, institutional and environmental barriers, excluding or hindering the subject's participation in the social environment. In this, it is affiliated with the social model of approaching disability as opposed to the medical model."

buildings and other facilities open to the public or for public use with signage in *Braille* and in easy-to-read and understand formats; *(iv)* offer forms of human or animal assistance and mediator services, including guides, readers and professional sign language interpreters, to facilitate access to buildings and other facilities open to the public or for public use; *etc.*

The disabled person was previously seen as someone who needed the protection of the state in every respect, someone who could not have autonomy over their own life, always needing the help of others to make decisions and participate in society. Since the Convention, member states have come to see the need to protect people with disabilities from the point of view of guaranteeing and promoting fundamental rights and individual freedoms.

To this end, they have committed themselves to bringing about changes in the social environment, eliminating barriers and guaranteeing reasonable adaptation as far as possible, so that people with disabilities can make decisions and participate fully in life in society, being able to self-determine.

People with disabilities can therefore demand that the state fulfil the duties laid down in the Convention, in order to guarantee their social inclusion through the realisation of various rights, such as accessibility and mobility.

In this regard, Taisa Maria Macena de Lima, Marcelo de Mello Vieira and Beatriz de Almeida Borges e Silva stand out:[70]

> People with disabilities are now treated materially as subjects of fundamental rights, and can demand the fulfilment of their right to be included in society, either to participate in society or to decide the direction of their own lives. In this way, people with disabilities are no longer waiting for charity from the state, but are entitled to their rights, which must be promoted through state public policies.

In this sense, accessibility is one of the general principles of the Convention, as can be seen from art. 3, point "f". Art. 20 of the Convention, in turn, deals specifically with the personal mobility of people with disabilities, assigning the following duties to States Parties: *(i)* facilitate the mobility of persons with disabilities, in the manner and at the time they wish, and at an affordable cost; *(ii)* facilitate access to quality assistive technologies, devices and technical aids, and forms of human or animal assistance and mediators, including by making them available at an affordable cost; *(Ui)* provide persons with disabilities and specialised personnel with training in mobility techniques; and *(iv)* encourage entities that produce mobility technical aids, devices and assistive technologies to take into account all aspects relating to the mobility of persons with disabilities.

In Article 24(3)(a), the Convention obliges States Parties to guarantee the education of people with disabilities, facilitating and encouraging their learning of orientation and mobility skills.

Article 30 of the Convention also relates to the right to mobility, in that it imposes a duty on States Parties to ensure that people with disabilities have access to cultural venues (such as theatres, museums, cinemas and libraries) and venues for sporting, recreational and leisure events, as well as a duty to encourage and promote the widest possible participation of people with disabilities in such activities.

In order to guarantee compliance with the provisions of the Convention, provision was made for the establishment of a Committee on the Rights of Persons with Disabilities to carry out the functions set out in the Convention, including: receiving and evaluating reports from states parties on the measures adopted to comply with the Convention and the progress made; drawing up reports on its activities; and making suggestions and general recommendations based on the reports of states parties, which will be submitted to the General Assembly and the Economic Council.

Together with the Convention, the Optional Protocol was created, which could or could not be signed by the

---

[70] LIMA, Maria Macena de Lima; VIEIRA, Marcelo de Mello; SILVA, Beatriz de Almeida Borges e. Reflexões sobre as pessoas com deficiência e sobre os impactos da Lei nº 13.146/2015 no estudo dos planos do negócio jurídico. *Brazilian Journal of Civil Law.* Belo Horizonte, vol. 14, p. 17-39, Oct./Dec. 2017

states parties to the Convention.

The signatories to the Protocol recognise the competence of the Committee on the Rights of Persons with Disabilities to receive and consider communications submitted by or on behalf of persons or groups of persons subject to its jurisdiction alleging that they are victims of violations of the provisions of the Convention by that State party. These communications can only be received if they concern States parties that are signatories to the Protocol.

The communications will be investigated confidentially and the co-operation of the state party will be requested, after which the result will be communicated to the state party, accompanied by suggestions and recommendations.

The Committee is therefore a body that monitors compliance with the provisions of the Convention by the states parties.

The representatives are elected by secret ballot from among those nominated by the States Parties from among their nationals, observing equitable geographical distribution, balanced representation of gender and of the different forms of civilisations and legal systems, as well as the participation of disability experts.

Brazil, a signatory to the Convention and the Optional Protocol, is subject to this scrutiny and, in June 2018, had its first representative elected to the United Nations Committee on the Rights of Persons with Disabilities (CRPD), Senator Mara Cristina Gabrilli.

3.3. The rights of people with disabilities in other countries after the UN Convention

At the *International Meeting on the Rights of Persons with Disabilities in the Private Law of Spain, Brazil, Italy and Portugal,* held on 29 and 30 January 2018 at the Faculty of Law of the University of Seville (Spain), several researchers presented the treatment that has been given in their respective countries to the rights of people with disabilities following the ratification of the UN Convention, as reported by Aline de Miranda Valverde Terra and Ana Carolina Brochado Teixeira[71] .

According to the authors, Fernando Araújo, Professor at the Faculty of Law of the University of Lisbon, said that in Portugal there was no legislative change after the Convention.

With regard to Italy, they report that two professors from the Faculty of Law at the University of Camerino, Agostina Latino and Maria Cristina de Cicco, have noted that, following the UN Convention, a law was passed establishing the figure of the *amministrazione di sostegno,* which aims to help people with disabilities in the administration and defence of their interests (Law No. 6 of 9 January 2004).

Finally, the authors report on the legislative changes and innovations that have taken place in Spain, as reported by researchers from that country:

> In Spain, Professor Dr Inmaculada Vivas-Tesón and notaries Almudena Castro-Girona Martínez and Manuel Seda Hermosín presented some important legislative changes - some of them even predating the ratification of the Convention - which introduced inter vivos and causa mortis instruments, some judicial and others extrajudicial, aimed at protecting people with disabilities. Among the inter vivos measures, they mentioned the prevenaquelas causa mortis, the establishment of a new cause of indignity to remove from the succession of the disabled person their relatives who have not provided them with the necessary assistance during their lifetime, and the establishment of a right of habitation over the habitual dwelling in favour of the disabled person.

Based on the reports of foreign researchers, it can be concluded that, in terms of legislative innovation, Brazil

---

[71] TERRA, Aline de Miranda Valverde; TEIXEIRA, Ana Carolina Brochado. Reflections from the 1st International Encounter on the Rights of Persons with Disabilities in the Private Law of Spain, Brazil, Italy and Portugal. *Brazilian Journal of Civil Law.* Belo Horizonte, vol. 15, p. 223-233, Jan./Mar. 2018.

has made great strides in protecting people with disabilities, specifically with the drafting of Law 13.146/2015,[72] which comprehensively protects the rights of such people, including accessibility, mobility and various other existential and property interests, in line with the provisions of the UN Convention.

25

---

[72] TERRA, Aline de Miranda Valverde; TEIXEIRA, Ana Carolina Brochado. Reflexões a partir do I Encuentro Internacional..., ob. cit.

CHAPTER 4

ACCESSIBILITY IN THE BRAZILIAN LAW ON THE INCLUSION OF PEOPLE WITH DISABILITIES

In Brazil, the Constitutions prior to the 1988 Constitution made little provision for people with disabilities, with the first mention only occurring in the 1967 Constitution, with Constitutional Amendment no. 01, and even then, the provisions were not very effective in practice. It was the 1988 Constitution that began to address more relevant changes to the rights and guarantees of these people[73] . Since then, there has been much greater concern for people with disabilities. There isn't an exclusive chapter or title to deal with their rights, but throughout the constitutional text it is possible to identify at least eleven provisions that specifically and directly protect these people.

It is important to note, on the other hand, that one of the foundations of the Federative Republic of Brazil is the dignity of the human person (art. I°) and that one of the fundamental objectives of the Republic is to "promote the good of all, without prejudice to origin, race, sex, colour, age or any other form of discrimination" (art. 3° , IV). Thus, it is understood that the 1988 Constitution aims to include everyone in life in society, which can be seen in the principle of equality (art. 5° , *capuf), which* also applies to people with disabilities. Therefore, this concern is not limited to specific articles, but surrounds the entire structure of the Constitution, even if progress has been slower in terms of reality. It is possible to point to the following other normative formulations in the Constitution aimed at protecting people with disabilities: art. 7° , XXXI; art. 23, II; art. 24, XIV; art. 37, VIII; art. 40, § I° , I and § 4° , I; art. 100, § 2° ; art. 201,1 and § I° ; art. 203, IV and V; art. 208, III; art. 227, § I° , II and § 2° , and art. 244. It is also worth mentioning art. 102, of the ADCT (Act of Transitory Constitutional Provisions), as a provision directly protecting people with disabilities.

Brazil gained greater relevance in the defence of the rights of people with disabilities after the enactment of Law No. 13.146/2015 (Brazilian Law for the Inclusion of People with Disabilities - Statute of People with Disabilities), which has been cited in other countries as an example of what can be done to comply with the Convention on the Rights of Persons with Disabilities.

The purpose of this law is to regulate the Convention and apply it more effectively at national level, since domestic legislation and the Constitution of the Republic itself predated the Convention.

Thus, Law 13.146/2015 adopted the new terminology and concepts brought about by the Convention on the Rights of Persons with Disabilities and amended some provisions of the Civil Code, the Code of Civil Procedure, as well as other laws on the subject. It also established new obligations and duties for all members of Brazilian society, including government entities and private legal entities.

4.1. Accessibility for people with disabilities.

Accessibility has been guaranteed by the 1988 Constitution of the Federative Republic of Brazil as a state policy since the document was promulgated.

> Art. 227 [...].
>
> § 20 The law will lay down standards for the construction of public places and buildings and for the manufacture of public transport vehicles, in order to guarantee adequate access for people with disabilities.
>
> [...].
>
> Art. 244: The law will provide for the adaptation of public places, buildings for public use and public transport vehicles currently in existence in order to guarantee adequate access for people with disabilities, in accordance with the provisions of art. 227, § 2° .

Law No. 10.048/2000, Law No. 10.098/2000 and Decree No. 5.296/2004 established the general rules on

---

[73] JAQUES, Karina. Fundamental right to accessibility, ob. cit. Accessed on: 19 Apr. 2017.

accessibility, with subsequent amendments promoted by Law No. 13.146/2015.

Accessibility consists of a set of works and measures that promote locomotion and access to public spaces for people with disabilities or reduced mobility.

The definition of a *person with a disability* is provided by legislation. Item I of § Iº of art. 5º of Decree no. 5.296/2004 defines such people as those who have a limitation or inability to perform an activity due to a disability. The same Decree considers there to be five types of disability: physical, hearing, visual, mental and multiple.

The Decree also establishes, in item II of § Iº of art. 5º , the conditions for someone to be considered a *person with reduced mobility*. This is an individual who does not have a physical, hearing, visual or mental disability, but who, for whatever reason, has difficulty moving around.

> Art. 5º . Direct, indirect and foundational public administration bodies, companies providing public services and financial institutions must give priority service to people with disabilities or reduced mobility.
>
> § 21   For the purposes of this Decree:
>
> I - disabled person, in addition to those provided for in Law 10.690 of 16 June 2003, who has a limitation or incapacity to perform an activity and falls into the following categories:
>
> a) physical disability: complete or partial alteration of one or more segments of the human body, leading to impairment of physical function, presenting itself in the form of paraplegia, paraparesis, monoplegia, monoparesis, tetraplegia, tetraparesis, triplegia, triparesis, hemiplegia, hemiparesis, ostomy, amputation or absence of limb, cerebral palsy, dwarfism, limbs with congenital or acquired deformity, except aesthetic deformities and those that do not produce difficulties for the performance of functions;
>
> b) hearing impairment: bilateral loss, partial or total, of forty-one decibels (dB) or more, measured by audiogram at 500Hz, 1,000Hz, 2,000Hz and 3,000Hz;
>
> c) Visual impairment: blindness, in which visual acuity is equal to or less than 0.05 in the better eye, with the best optical correction; low vision, which means visual acuity between 0.3 and 0.05 in the better eye, with the best optical correction; cases in which the sum of the visual field measurements in both eyes is equal to or less than 60o; or the simultaneous occurrence of any of the above conditions;
>
> d) mental disability: intellectual functioning significantly below average, with manifestation before the age of eighteen and limitations associated with two or more areas of adaptive skills, such as:
>
> 1. communication;
>
> 2. personal care;
>
> 3. social skills;
>
> 4. use of community resources;
>
> 5. health and safety;
>
> 6. academic skills;
>
> 7. leisure; and
>
> 8. work;
>
> e) multiple disability - association of two or more disabilities; and
>
> II - a person with reduced mobility means a person who does not fall within the concept of a disabled person but who, for whatever reason, has difficulty moving around, either permanently or temporarily, resulting in an effective reduction in mobility, flexibility, motor coordination and perception.

In a similar vein, Law No. 13.146/2015 (Statute of Persons with Disabilities) also defines persons with disabilities and persons with reduced mobility. According to the *caput of* art. 2º , a person with a disability is "someone who has a long-term physical, mental, intellectual or sensory impairment which, in interaction with one or more barriers, may obstruct their full and effective participation in society on equal terms with other people". And item IX of art. 3º defines a person with reduced mobility as "anyone who has, for whatever reason, permanent or temporary difficulty in moving, generating an effective reduction in mobility, flexibility, motor coordination or perception, including the elderly, pregnant women, nursing mothers, people with infants and obese people".

Public spaces are understood to include not only the public goods provided for in articles 98 to 103 of the Civil Code. It is a generic expression that covers the assets of legal entities governed by public law, as well as private assets that are geared towards some activity for the public.

Chapters IV (arts. 11 to 12-A) and V (arts. 13 to 15) of Law No. 10.098/2000 establish general accessibility standards for buildings for private use and for public buildings or buildings for collective use. They therefore cover all buildings that are intended for the general public:

> Art. 11: The construction, extension or remodelling of public or private buildings intended for collective use must be carried out in such a way that they are or become accessible to people with disabilities or reduced mobility.
>
> [...].

In this sense, art. 8º of Decree no. 5.296/2004 creates an *obligatio ob rem of* accessibility (*propter rem obligation)* for properties used by the public. See also the definitions in sections VI, VII and VIII, *in verbis*

Public buildings	Collective use buildings	Buildings for private use
Those administered by direct and indirect public administration entities, or by	Those intended for commercial, hotel, cultural, sporting and financial activities,	Those intended for residential use, which can be classified as single-family or multi-family.
companies providing public services and aimed at the general public.	Tourist, recreational, social, religious, educational, industrial and health buildings, including buildings providing services for activities of the same nature.	

For example, a restaurant or bar is the private property of its owner and cannot be considered a public asset as defined in Article 98 of the Civil Code. However, the activity carried out in that establishment is intended for the public, which is why the property, even if private, is considered a public space. It is therefore subject to the duty to promote accessibility for those who need it.

Furthermore, it should be borne in mind that in Brazil the owners of private establishments engaged in business and commercial activities do not have the so-called *"right to refuse service"*.

The *right to refuse service, which* originated in the United States, consists of the right of the owner of a commercial establishment to refuse to provide a service or supply a product to a consumer.

In Brazilian consumer law, any kind of discrimination is forbidden, so the supplier has no similar rights here. Incidentally, article 39, IX of the CDC considers it an abusive practice to "refuse to sell goods or provide services directly to anyone willing to purchase them upon prompt payment, except in cases of intermediation regulated by special laws". However, considering the supplier's duty to guarantee the integrity of the consumer, he can refuse to serve and allow in people who, anomalously, put other consumers and users at risk. (But, you see, in this case it won't be a right to refuse, but a *duty to refuse).*

In this sense, as a reinforcing element of conviction, we cite the opinion of the Iª Chamber of Private Law of the São Paulo State Court of Justice[74] :

---

[74] TJSP, APL 0003271-31.2011.8.26.0390 SP 0003271-31.2011.8.26.0390, Iª Câmara de Direito Privado, Rei. Alcides Leopoldo e Silva Júnior, j. on 01/12/2015. The same understanding was used in another judgement: TJSP, AI 2056278-

> Although it is not a case of discrimination or prejudice based on race, colour, ethnicity, religion or national origin, there are some situations in which it is lawful to refuse service to customers *(Right to Refuse Service), to* prevent entry to establishments and events open to the public - Absence of unlawfulness in the conduct of the event's security team, given the risk of a renewed clash between the confronting groups, putting the safety and physical safety of the public at risk - Legitimate preventive measure - Unjust moral damage not characterised.

The Federal Supreme Court, in a monocratic decision handed down in AI no. 812.980/RJ, upheld the ruling of the Rio de Janeiro State Court of Justice which recognised the exercise of the *right to refuse service* against a customer who put the integrity of the establishment's employees and other customers at risk[75] :

> DECISION: (1) This is an interlocutory appeal against a decision rejecting the processing of an extraordinary appeal against a judgement of the Rio de Janeiro Court of Justice, which reads as follows: "Civil appeal. Obligation not to do. The complexity of social relations in today's context requires the interpreter to compare the rules protecting individual rights with those designed to preserve collective interests. In post-modern times, the individual is the radiating centre of normative parameters, but the exercise of personal rights is in competition with the preservation of rights that emerge from inescapable and necessary social coexistence. Thus, those who are unfit to do so cannot, by invoking their right to come and go, prevent the peaceful coexistence of others. An individual who goes into a commercial establishment full of customers, assaults the staff and puts the integrity of the others present at risk, causing a huge uproar by promoting a break-in. Precedents in comparative law can be found in the *Right to Refuse Service,* which faces the limitations set out in the *Civil Right Act of 1964.* In our legal system, the rules regulating consumer relations (Law 8.078/90) require business owners to take all measures to ensure the physical integrity of employees and visitors to their premises, and the owner of the establishment's claim to prevent anyone from entering who poses a risk to the development of their commercial activities is legitimate. Obligation not to do with which the debtor can be compelled to comply by means of *a vis aflictiva* set at an amount compatible with the context. The appeal is partially upheld." [...]. It can be seen that the lower court recognised, in light of the facts considered in the light of the evidence, that the owner of the commercial establishment's intention to prevent anyone who posed a risk to the premises and its customers from entering was legitimate. It's enough to read what the ruling says: "(...) All things considered, it must be concluded that, if the business owner is obliged to take all measures to ensure the physical integrity of his employees and those who frequent his premises, it must also be recognised as legitimate for him to prevent the entry of those who pose a risk to the development of his commercial activities (...)". To disagree with these factual assessments that led to the decisive content of the judgement would require a re-examination of facts and evidence, in the light of which the case was decided, which is forbidden in the extraordinary instance (Precedent 279).

What risk can a wheelchair user, a blind person or a deaf person pose to the integrity and safety of users of private spaces for collective use? Incidentally, it is against this stigma that the Statute of the Person with Disabilities arises, creating precepts and duties that promote - albeit in the long term - a change of perception in relation to those with disabilities[76] .

Accessibility is therefore a duty that applies to public or private buildings for collective use. It also affects multi-family environments (such as condominiums), public places, furniture, communications and

---

02.2014.8.26.0000 SP 2056278-02.2014.8.26.0000, Iª Câmara de Direito Privado, Rei. Alcides Leopoldo e Silva Júnior, j. on 24/05/2014.

[75] STF, AI n°. 812.980/RJ, King. Cezar Peluso, j. 03/08/2012.

[76] Regarding awareness of the inclusion of people with disabilities, VALIM, Rosangela Valim; TIOZZO, Arnaldo Ap. Acessibilidade: do direito a função social. In: *Revista Pandora Brasil,* n° 26, January 2011: "But the benefits guaranteed by the Laws are not [szc] synonymous with awareness. We still see that many citizens who have the right to differentiated services don't go to the streets, bars, stadiums, galleries, fairs, schools, concerts, stadiums, etc. because they realise that they are different. And what are we doing to change that? Not much. We know how necessary and important it is to change our behaviour and discourse. We know that there are different people among us. But we don't accept it. We consider these citizens to be 'unfamiliar' to us."

signposting.

These are examples of adaptations that provide accessibility:

- tactile flooring for pavements;
- crossings;
- handrails;
- ramps;
- tactile floors;
- urban buildings;
- adapting street furniture to specific standards;
- signalling street crossings;
- lifts;
- suspension platforms; and
- audible warnings at traffic lights and on public transport.

Difficulties in getting around and accessing certain environments, however, are not the only ones faced by this section of the population. Accessibility seeks to eliminate or reduce all types of barriers and obstacles faced by people with disabilities or reduced mobility, and this includes access to information and communication, as well as their public and political participation.

In this sense, the Statute for Persons with Disabilities, in line with the UN Convention on the Rights of Persons with Disabilities, addresses the concept of barriers in art. 3º , IV:

> barriers: any impediment, obstacle, attitude or behaviour that limits or prevents a person's social participation, as well as the enjoyment, fruition and exercise of their rights to accessibility, freedom of movement and expression, communication, access to information, understanding, safe movement, among others, classified as:
>
> a) urban barriers: those existing on roads and in public and private spaces open to the public or for collective use;
>
> b) architectural barriers: those existing in public and private buildings;
>
> c) barriers in transport: those existing in transport systems and means;
>
> d) communication and information barriers: any obstacle, attitude or behaviour that makes it difficult or impossible to express or receive messages and information through communication and information technology systems;
>
> e) attitudinal barriers: attitudes or behaviours that prevent or hinder the social participation of people with disabilities on equal terms and opportunities with other people;
>
> f) technological barriers: those that hinder or prevent people with disabilities from accessing technology;

It is also possible to divide these barriers into a tripartite classification, namely: 1) attitudinal barriers, represented by fear, ignorance and low expectations; 2) environmental barriers, resulting from the physical inaccessibility of the surroundings; and 3) institutional barriers, which are legally backed discriminations that justify the exclusion of certain rights for people with disabilities.[77]

These concepts confirm the idea that accessibility is for all people with disabilities or reduced mobility, not just those with walking difficulties, but also individuals with speech, visual, cognitive and hearing disorders and all other possible differences that, in contact with these barriers, prevent them from living their full lives. This is because accessibility must be seen as a broad concept that encompasses the elimination of all the aforementioned types of barriers, which is achieved by adapting the environment so that it can be used and accessed by all people, regardless of any type of physical attribute capable of generating difficulties or

---

[77] MENEZES, Joyceane Bezerra de; MENEZES, Herika Janaynna Bezerra de; MENEZES, Abraão Bezerra de. The approach to disability in the face of the expansion of human rights, ob. cit.

impediments to access when in contact with such barriers.

In an effort to realise accessibility, the Brazilian Association of Technical Standards (ABNT) created NBR 9050:2015, which is the Standard for Accessibility to Buildings, Furniture, Spaces and Urban Equipment, with the aim of establishing parameters and technical criteria to be observed in the preparation of projects, constructions, installations and adaptations of buildings, as well as furniture, spaces and urban equipment to the conditions of accessibility, indicating specifications that aim to provide the safe use of the environment or equipment to the largest possible number of people, regardless of age, height or mobility limitation (ABNT NBR 9050:2015). This confirms the assertion that not only the government has a responsibility to ensure the inclusion of people with disabilities, but that this is the duty of society as a whole, in order to reduce the difficulties faced by these individuals.

In Brazil, accessibility is also defined by legislation:

Law no. 10.098/2000	Decree no. 5.296/2004	Law 13.146/2015
Art. 2º . [...]. I - accessibility: the possibility and condition of being able to safely and autonomously use spaces , furniture, equipment urban areas, buildings, transport, information and communication, including their systems and technologies, as well as other services and facilities open to the public, for public or private use, both in urban and rural areas, for people with disabilities or reduced mobility; [...].	Art. 8º . [...]. I - accessibility: condition for the safe and autonomous use, total or assisted, of the spaces, furniture and urban equipment, buildings, transport services and communication and information devices, systems and media, for people with disabilities or reduced mobility;	Art. 3 [...]. I - accessibility: the possibility and condition of being able to safely and autonomously use spaces , furniture, equipment urban areas, buildings, transport, information and communication, including their systems and technologies, as well as other services and facilities open to the public, for public or private use, both in urban and rural areas, for people with disabilities or reduced mobility; [--]- Art. 53: Accessibility is a right that guarantees that people with disabilities or reduced mobility can live independently and exercise their rights to citizenship and social participation.

Note that in the last 15 years, accessibility has gone from being a technical concept of overcoming barriers to becoming a special attribute for the exercise of citizenship and the personality of people with disabilities. This, by the way, is the meaning given to accessibility by Luiz Alberto David Araújo and Maurício Maia, when analysing the constitutional provision of duty[78] :

> In fact, without accessibility, people with disabilities (and other groups, such as people with reduced mobility) would be, if not prevented, seriously handicapped in the exercise of practically all their fundamental rights, being excluded from social participation. How can we enjoy the right to work without guaranteeing a working environment that can accommodate people with disabilities, allowing them access to all their spaces? How can you enjoy the right to education if you don't allow people with disabilities to move around the school environment? What's more, how can you exercise any of your rights if cities and public transport are not prepared to welcome people with disabilities?

In this sense, accessibility is no longer a set of technical rules, but a value inherent to the personal condition.

---

[78] ARAÚJO, Luiz Alberto David; MAIA, Maurício. The city, the constitutional duty of social inclusion and accessibility. In: *Revista de Direito da Cidade,* vol. 08, nº 1. Rio de Janeiro, 2016, pp. 230-231. BENTES, Hilda Helena Soares. Hephaestus able: from myth to the rights of people with disabilities. In: *Revista Jurídica da Presidência Brasília,* v. 19, n. 118, Jun./Sept. 2017, pp. 352-376.

In this way, it becomes a personality right.

Much progress still needs to be made in implementing full accessibility. An example of this is the empirical study carried out by a team from the Civil Engineering course at the Federal University of Pará (UFPA), made up of Allan Veiga Brito Tourinho, Brenno Pires Percy, Camila Pereira Oliveira, Ricardo Julio Dos Santos Gaspar and Rita De Cassia Monteiro Moraes, in which they qualitatively analysed Avenida Duque de Caxias, located in the city of Belém do Pará[79] .

The researchers found that, despite the revitalisation of the avenue in 2007, there is still a need for constant maintenance of pavements, signs and access ramps, as the evaluation found a significant number of non-compliances. The researchers concluded:

> After carrying out the checks, we realised that the avenue, despite having been designed as a road adapted to make it easier for people with some kind of restriction to get around, has several design and executive flaws. Some of these even make it impossible to move along the pavement, making it necessary to use the carriageway to overcome obstacles. We would also highlight the lack of supervision and guidance given to residents in the area to ensure that they correctly carry out maintenance and repairs on the pavements for which they are responsible. Unfortunately, at the end of this study, we can say that it is impracticable to travel safely along the entire road, and in some stretches it is impossible for people with physical restrictions.

Another example of empirical research that detected similar difficulties was carried out by Suelen Aparecida Felicetti, Angelita Gralak Bemardine, Zulméia Carteli and Sandro Aparecido dos Santos. Through empirical studies of specific cases, the researchers analysed what five people who are blind or have low vision think about the accessibility conditions of buildings.

public spaces in the city of Guarapuava, in the state of Paraná. They also investigated how this interferes with the orientation and mobility of blind people.

The researchers realised that the streets, crossings and public transport do not meet accessibility requirements. They also realised that these requirements are essential for the development of orientation and mobility. There is a lack of tactile flooring, the pavements are uneven, there is a lack of audible traffic lights and public transport. They conclude: "The analyses of the reports show that all these accessibility resources are lacking in public spaces in the city of Guarapuava/PR. As a result, they are unable to find their way around safely and autonomously on their own, which is detrimental to their independence."[80] .

That's right. The truth is that this is the reality in many Brazilian cities. Despite all the rules and laws that govern the matter, looking at the reality of Brazilian society, it is currently clear that the desired ideal is far from being fully achieved. It is easy to see in everyday life the difficulties faced by people with disabilities, and even those with reduced mobility. These difficulties include uneven pavements and no access ramps to the streets, places where car parking spaces are not properly reserved, public transport with faulty lifts for wheelchair users, universities, schools and even health centres and hospitals that do not have ramps, lifts or accessible toilets for these people.

Another difficulty is the lack of empathy and respect on the part of a large part of the population, which to this day does not comply with the rules guaranteeing the rights of people with disabilities, for example when they use spaces specially designated for them, such as spaces reserved for cars whose owner has a disability or is elderly. Another common example is non-compliance with accessibility standards in private environments for

---

[79] TOURINHO, Allan Veiga Brito; PERCY, Brenno Pires; OLIVEIRA, Camila Pereira; GASPAR, Ricardo Julio Dos Santos; MORAES, Rita De Cassia Monteiro. Evaluation of traffic conditions and accessibility on pavements. In: *Multidisciplinary Scientific Journal-Nucleus of Knowledge*. Year 03, ed. 10, vol. 03, pp. 51-63, October 2018.
[80] FELICETTI, Suelen Aparecida; BERNARDINE, Angelita Gralak; CARTELI, Zulméia; SANTOS, Sandro Aparecido dos. Accessibility, orientation and mobility: a case study from the point of view of people who are blind or have low vision. In: *Divers@ Interdisciplinary Electronic Journal*. Matinhos, v. 9, n. 1, pp. 39- 51, jan./dez. 2016, p. 40.

collective use, such as residential condominiums.

All of this hinders - and sometimes prevents - the full and independent lives of people with disabilities, who need help to do simple things like walk the streets of the city they live in and even access their own homes.

4.2. Accessibility as a personality right.

The Statute aims to give people with disabilities a dignified life. The proposed new concept of disability goes beyond the limits of personal conditions and is now determined on the basis of the worsening of natural limitations due to social barriers. In this sense, it is up to society to rehabilitate itself in order to reduce these barriers and allow people to participate fully in society.[81]

Disability does not exist on its own; it arises from the interaction between the specific attributes of the person and the barriers of the environment, which hinder or prevent access to spaces, the development of work, mobility and the exercise of rights[82] .

Inclusion is only possible through accessibility, which is also responsible for giving people with disabilities a dignified life. For this reason, accessibility should be considered a personality right.

Personality rights, in the view of Alexandre Cortez Femandes, are rights related to the protection of the human person, considered essential to their dignity and integrity. He also states that they are faculties exercised naturally by the person, being an attribute of the human condition[83] .

It so happens that the merely exemplary list provided for in the Civil Code does not exhaust the objective of personality rights, which is the full protection of the person in all their biopsychological, spiritual and intellectual aspects. It is for this reason that there is a general clause for the protection of personality, which has as its logical presupposition art. Iº , III, of the CRFB/88, i.e. the dignity of the human person[84] . Francisco Amaral states that respect for the human person is the basic legal framework that justifies the existence and allows the specification of other rights[85] .

The constant transformations in society create new situations on a daily basis, giving rise to the need to protect aspects not covered by the legal text and often not even imaginable in other times.

So, if the aim of personality rights is to protect the dignity of the human person by safeguarding all aspects of it, it is easy to see that other rights, even if they are not provided for in the 2002 Civil Code, can be included as personality rights, as long as they are necessary for the human condition, i.e. they must be an attribute of the personality.

That said, the accessibility provided for in Law No. 13.146/2015 must be understood as a right of the personality, as it appears as an instrument for the exercise of citizenship by people with disabilities, as Luiz Alberto David Araújo and Maurício Maia point out: "In the case of people with disabilities, citizenship cannot be thought of without accessibility, there would be no equality if they were not guaranteed accessibility, which

---

[81] MENEZES, Joyceane Bezerra de; MENEZES, Herika Janaynna Bezerra de; MENEZES, Abraão Bezerra de. The approach to disability in the face of the expansion of human rights, ob. cit.

[82] FERRAZ, Carolina Valença; LEITE, Glauber Salomão. Brazilian inclusion law and the "new" concept of disability: will it "catch on" now? Available at: <http://justificando.cartacapital.com.br/2015/08/20/lei- brasileira-de-inclusao-e-o-novo-conceito-de-de-deficiencia-sera-que-agora-vai-pegar/>. Accessed on: 13 June 2017. FELICETTI, Suelen Aparecida; BERNARDINE, Angelita Gralak; CARTELI, Zulméia; SANTOS, Sandro Aparecido dos. Accessibility, orientation and mobility: a case study from the point of view of people who are blind or have low vision, ob. cit: "Poor accessibility affects the quality of life, independence, access to public places and leisure for people who are blind or have low vision. It is impossible for them to develop orientation and mobility in a public space without, for example, tactile flooring or regular pavements. This lack of accessibility often goes unnoticed in society, just like blindness and low vision themselves. It seems that what is different from the imposed standards is ignored, just as the existence of prejudice and discrimination is ignored."

[83] FERNANDES, Alexandre Cortez. *Civil Law. Introduction: people and property.* Caxias do Sul: EDUCS, 2012, p. 192.

[84] FARIAS, Cristiano Chaves de; ROSENVALD, Nelson. *Civil Law: General Theory.* 6ª ed. Rio de Janeiro: Lumen Juris, 2007, p. 116.

[85] AMARAL, Francisco. *Civil Law: Introduction.* 7ª ed. Rio de Janeiro: Renovar, 2008, p. 292.

is, in addition to a right in itself, a necessary prerequisite for the enjoyment of all fundamental rights by people with disabilities. There will only be real inclusion if accessibility is guaranteed"[86].

According to Luiz Alberto David Araújo and Waldir Macieira da Costa Filho[87], the interpretation of art. 3°, I, of Law no. 13.146/2015, in line with the concept of person with a disability in the *heading of* art. 2° of the same law, leads to the perception that:

> physical, sensory, mental and intellectual impediments do not produce obstacles on their own, but rather these barriers that prevent the exercise of rights are produced socially, and political, legal and social strategies are essential to exclude these obstacles and negative discrimination, allowing disabled people to demonstrate their abilities and enjoy autonomy and independence for real social inclusion.

The exclusion of socially produced barriers takes place, among other things, through accessibility, which not only seeks to include people with disabilities, but also those with "reduced mobility", including the elderly, pregnant women, nursing mothers, people with infants and the obese (art. 3°, IX, of Law no. 13.146/2015).

In this sense, the Statute for People with Disabilities initially states that it is the duty of the state, society and the family to ensure that people with disabilities enjoy all the rights enshrined in the Constitution, including accessibility:

> Art. 8°. It is the duty of the state, society and the family to ensure that people with disabilities, as a matter of priority, have their rights to life, health, sexuality, paternity and maternity, food, housing, education, vocational training, work, social security, habilitation and rehabilitation, transport, accessibility, culture, sport, tourism, leisure, information, communication, scientific and technological advances, dignity, respect, freedom, family and community coexistence, among others arising from the Federal Constitution, the Convention on the Rights of Persons with Disabilities and its Optional Protocol and the laws and other norms that guarantee their personal, social and economic well-being.

However, the Statute has given this rule a clear outline by laying out each fundamental right and the way in which each one should be realised. In addition, it used an entire title of this law (arts. 53 to 76) to discuss accessibility in all its versions, since when it comes to fundamental rights, simply reading the provisions leads to the conclusion that without accessibility it would not be possible to realise them.

Furthermore, it can be seen that the law not only established guarantees for people with disabilities on a formal level, but also laid down rules imposing obligations on both the state and individuals and companies, and brought new elements to demand, with greater rigour, compliance with these guarantees on a factual level[88].

---

[86] ARAÚJO, Luiz Alberto David; MAIA, Maurício. The city, the constitutional duty of social inclusion and accessibility, ob. cit.

[87] ARAÚJO, Luiz Alberto David; COSTA FILHO, Waldir Macieira da. The statute for people with disabilities - EPCD (Law no. 13.146, of 06.07.2015): some new features. In: *Revista dos Tribunais,* vol. 962, pp. 65-80, Dec/2015, p. 65.

[88] ARAÚJO, Luiz Alberto David; COSTA FILHO, Waldir Macieira da. O estatuto da pessoa com deficiência - EPCD..., ob. cit. With specific regard to public authorities, duties were imposed in order to guarantee compliance with accessibility requirements in public and private works for collective use, as well as in public transport and electronic sites, thus making it clear that the state is more responsible for ensuring that the rights of people with disabilities and reduced mobility are realised with regard to their mobility, access to information, communication and participation in public and political life. An important innovation in this area was the amendment to Article 11, IX of Law No. 8.429/92, which now considers it an act of administrative improbity that violates the principles of public administration to "fail to comply with the accessibility requirements set out in the legislation", i.e. any action or omission by the state that results in the failure to guarantee accessibility for people with disabilities is now an act of improbity, which reinforces the idea of the law to ensure that these rights are not restricted to the formal level. This, however, was not the only novelty in this regard; changes were also made to the Tenders Law (Law no. 8.666/93) in order to require compliance with accessibility standards and establishing the administration's obligation to monitor compliance with accessibility requirements in services and

Article 53 of Law 13.146/2015 provides for accessibility as a right that guarantees people with disabilities or reduced mobility the right to live independently and exercise their rights to citizenship and social participation. The lack of accessibility means that these citizens suffer the restriction of numerous rights, including the exercise of their own citizenship, which in a democratic society is unacceptable. Obviously, a life with so many restrictions can in no way be considered dignified. In this sense, Luiz Alberto David Araújo and Maurício Maia write: "Accessibility is a necessary prerequisite for the inclusion of people with disabilities, a vulnerable group that represents almost a quarter of the national population, who, without accessibility, are prevented, or seriously impaired, in the enjoyment of practically all their fundamental rights"[89] .

Accessibility is a personality right because it is necessary to guarantee dignity and is essential for the full exercise and development of the personality. Only through accessibility will people with disabilities or reduced mobility be able to exercise all the faculties inherent to their personality, such as freedom of movement, the right to information, communication and all the other fundamental rights of the human person.

As Mara Gabrilli writes, "it is very important to understand that when we talk about accessibility, we are referring to the right of every citizen to come and go". That's why she emphasises that "accessibility is much more than building a ramp", and testifies to the importance of accessibility in the life of a disabled person[90] :

> As well as making us worthy, access brings us happiness. After all, it is through accessibility that we find ways to make our work, leisure and study routines possible. So we can say that without access we don't have the opportunity to exercise our citizenship. And nobody is happy without it.

The legal system must therefore protect accessibility as a right of the personality, so that its violation gives rise to the due responsibility of the person who harmed it, to compensate for the damage caused to the disabled person.

---

work environments (art. 66-A, sole paragraph), as well as others.

[89] ARAÚJO, Luiz Alberto David; MAIA, Maurício. The city, the constitutional duty of social inclusion and accessibility, ob. cit.

[90] GABRILLI, Mara. Accessibility is much more than building a ramp. In: *Pandora Brasil Magazine*, n° 26, January 2011. Mara Cristina Gabrilli suffered a car accident in 1994 which left her with permanent quadriplegia, which is why she gets around in a wheelchair. She was a São Paulo City Councillor (2007-2011), a Federal Deputy (2011-2019) and is a Senator (2019-2027). She was São Paulo's first Secretary for People with Disabilities and Reduced Mobility.

CHAPTER 5

PROCEDURAL PROTECTION OF THE RIGHT TO ACCESSIBILITY

With the advent of ethical personalism, man was placed at the centre of the legal system, so that his rights were fully protected, giving greater importance to fundamental and personality rights.

In this context, moral damage is now considered a consequence of the unlawful act in the civil sphere as well, and is conceptualised, in the strict sense, as a violation of the right to dignity. In other words: moral damage is injury to personality rights.

Nowadays, it is not necessarily linked to aspects of suffering, pain, or any other psychic reaction of the victim as a requirement for the configuration of moral damage, and there may be a violation of dignity without necessarily having such reactions, and vice versa.

This chapter will show that the absence of adaptations that provide accessibility - here referred to as *inaccessibility* - constitutes a genuine unlawful act (art. 186 of the Civil Code), which results in the civil liability of the agent responsible for the inaccessibility.

5.1. Inaccessibility as an injury to the personality of people with disabilities.

The concept of moral damage and the ways in which it can be redressed has undergone various changes over the years. Sérgio Cavalieri Filho states that there are various currents. For example, there are those who claim that it is a negative concept, with moral damage being that which does not have a patrimonial character. On the other hand, there is a positive concept, which defines moral damage as pain, vexation, suffering, discomfort, humiliation, in other words, "pain of the soul". The victim's psychological reaction can only constitute moral damage when it is related to an aggression against their dignity[91] .

In the same vein, Maria Celina Bodin de Moraes states[92][93] :

> Individuals have very personal rights that are part of their personality and have no economic connotations. Damage to these rights has been called moral, because it affects the valued attributes, or virtues, of the person as a social entity, i.e. integrated into society.

It is unacceptable to think that an injustice committed by someone, violating the personality rights of others, could be ignored in the legal sphere. Thus, moral damage is compensated in cash as an indemnity for the injury to the victim's dignity.

For Maria Celina Bodin de Moraes, it is not the pain that is being paid for, but the victim, who has been damaged in their off-balance sheet sphere, who is being compensated for the injury. Thus, the victim will be able to enjoy other states of psycho-physical well-being, in order to offset the effects that the damage has had on their spirit.

The situations that give rise to moral damage, therefore, are mainly based on the violation of human dignity, as well as the suffering caused to the victim, but this is not a necessary precondition for the existence of the damage.

With the passage of time, there has been an increase in the chances of causing damage, so that harmful situations that had previously been ignored have come to be protected on the basis of the principle of human dignity. Among these new causes of moral damage, it is possible to include a violation of the right to accessibility, since inaccessibility affects people with disabilities or reduced mobility in their personal sphere,

---

[91] CAVALIERI FILHO, Sérgio. *Civil Liability Programme.* 11ª ed. São Paulo: Atlas, 2014, pp. 106- 107.
[92] MORAES, Maria Celina Bodin de. *Damages to the Human Person.* Rio de Janeiro: Renovar, 2013, p. 155.
[93] MORAES, Maria Celina Bodin de. *Danos à Pessoa Humana,* ob. cit.

making it impossible for them to exercise their citizenship and basic rights to a full life in society[94] .

Furthermore, with the advent of the new Brazilian Inclusion Law, accessibility is now treated as a personality right and moral damage is nothing more than a violation of personality rights or, in the strict sense, the dignity of the human person.

When it comes to violating the right to accessibility, there is a clear violation of human dignity, since without accessibility, people with disabilities or reduced mobility are unable to enjoy a dignified life, and find themselves unable to exercise their fundamental rights, to be independent and also to have full social inclusion, which would only be possible if the principle of equality were respected.

For this reason, the violation of the right to accessibility must be repaired through compensation for moral damage, which must be assessed by the court in the specific case, evaluating the seriousness of the damage in view of the victim's personal conditions[95] .

Anyone whose right to accessibility is violated has the right to compensation for the moral damage resulting from the injury.

The existence of moral damage is established by proof of the harmful event, i.e. moral damage exists *in re ipsa,* deriving from the offensive event itself[96] . Thus, in the case of damage resulting from inaccessibility, it is enough to prove the damaging fact, i.e. the lack of accessibility that prevents the victim from exercising some right. There is therefore no need to talk about proving the person's suffering, since the fact in itself already constitutes a violation of the human dignity of the person with a disability or reduced mobility. In other words, moral damage arises from the simple violation of a personality right, namely accessibility.

Some Brazilian court judgements show that inaccessibility was already being treated as a cause that could give rise to compensation for moral damages. Decisions were made on the basis of laws that already regulated certain accessibility standards, as well as the UN Convention on the Rights of Persons with Disabilities. See the following judgement[97] :

> ACTION FOR COMPENSATION FOR MORAL DAMAGES PHYSICALLY DISABLED SPECIAL SEAT NOT MADE AVAILABLE. Claim to have the order to pay compensation for moral damages cancelled or reduced. INADMISSIBLE: The airline company has not produced any proof that there was no fault in the provision of the service or the exclusive fault of the consumer or third parties. The compensation was set at a reasonable and proportional amount. Judgement upheld. APPEAL DISMISSED.

The Superior Court of Justice has already recognised the right to compensation for inaccessibility[98] :

> INTERLOCUTORY APPEAL IN SPECIAL APPEAL. CONSUMER LAW AND CIVIL PROCEDURE (CPC/73). PHYSICAL DISABILITY (DWARFISM). INABILITY TO ACCESS THE VALIDATOR DEVICE OF THE ELECTRONIC TICKETING SYSTEM. [...]. 5 - QUANTUM OF COMPENSATION FOR MORAL DAMAGES. ARTICLE 944 OF THE CC. REASONABILITY. ADEQUACY TO THE SPECIFIC CASE. IMPOSSIBILITY OF REDUCTION. SÚMULA 07/STJ. 6 - JURISPRUDENTIAL DISAGREEMENT. NOT PROVEN. 7 - APPEAL DISMISSED.

In another judgement, the Superior Court of Justice established the following understanding[99] :

> Special appeal. Public civil action. Action aimed at imposing on the defendant financial institution the obligation to adopt the Braille method in bank contracts entered into with visually impaired

---

[94] MORAES, Maria Celina Bodin de. *Danos à Pessoa Humana,* ob. cit.

[95] SCHREIBER, Anderson. *Rights of Personality.* São Paulo: Atlas, 2011, p. 17.

[96] CAVALIERI FILHO, Sérgio. *Civil Liability Programme,* ob. cit.

[97] TJ-SP, APL n° 00353737220128260002 SP 0035373-72.2012.8.26.0002, 37ª Chamber of Private Law, King. Judge Israel Góes dos Anjos, j. on 02/04/2013.

[98] STJ, AgInt no AREsp n° 914.578/RJ, 3ª Turma, Rei. Min. Paulo de Tarso Sanseverino, j. on 09/03/2017.

[99] STJ, REsp n° 1.315.822/RJ, 3ª Turma, Rei. Marco Aurélio Bellizze, j. on 24/03/2015.

persons. 1) Formation of a necessary passive joint venture. Legal obligation to use the Braille method in banking contracts with visually impaired consumers. Existence. Constitutional and legal normativity. Observance. Necessary. 3. condemnation for collective extra-patrimonial damage. Appropriate. 4. imposition of a daily fine for non-compliance with court orders. Revision of the amount set. Necessary in this case. 5. effects of the judgement handed down in a public civil action aimed at protecting collective interests stricto sensu. Decision that produces effects in relation to all visually impaired consumers who have entered into or will enter into a contractual relationship with the defendant financial institution throughout the national territory. Indivisibility of the right protected. Article 16 of Law 7.347/1985. Inapplicable in this case. Precedents. [Special appeal partially granted.

From all the above, we can see the essential role of the courts in making the right to accessibility a reality, since not only is it possible to claim compensation for moral damages, but it is also possible to demand compliance with accessibility standards.

After the Statute for Persons with Disabilities came into force, some judgements began to understand inaccessibility as a wrongful act, from which the duty to compensate for moral damage arises.

This is what happened in the Superior Court of Justice, as can be seen in Special Appeal No. 1.733.468/MG. Note that the moral damage that can be compensated stems from the inaccessibility itself, and not from some reflexive embarrassment[100] :

> CIVIL LAW. SPECIAL APPEAL. ACTION FOR COMPENSATION FOR MORAL DAMAGES. FAILURE TO PROVIDE MUNICIPAL PUBLIC TRANSPORT SERVICE. DISABLED PERSON USING A MOTORISED WHEELCHAIR. LACK OF ACCESSIBILITY. DISCRIMINATORY TREATMENT BY THE CONCESSIONAIRE'S STAFF. MOTION FOR CLARIFICATION. OMISSION, CONTRADICTION, OBSCURITY OR MATERIAL ERROR. ABSENT. ANALYSIS OF LOCAL LAW. UNVIABLE. VIOLATION OF THE SERVICE USER'S RIGHT TO TRANSPORT AND MOBILITY. MORAL DAMAGE ESTABLISHED. AMOUNT SET BY THE COURT OF ORIGIN. APPROPRIATE. SUCCUMBENCE FEES. INCREASED. (2) The purpose of the appeal, beyond the denial of judicial service, is to assess the reasonableness of the amount set by the court of origin as compensation for moral damages to the defendant, for having been neglected and discriminated against as a person with a physical disability, when using urban public transport buses. [The International Convention on the Rights of Persons with Disabilities - which has been incorporated into the national legal system with the status of a constitutional amendment - has made accessibility a general principle to be observed by the States Parties, and has also given it the character of a fundamental human right, under the view that disability is not a problem in the person to be cured, but a problem in society, which imposes barriers that limit or even prevent the full performance of social roles (the so-called "social model of disability"). [Accessibility in public transport is of nodal importance for the effective inclusion of people with disabilities, as it allows them to exercise their citizenship and individual rights and freedoms, connecting them to places of work, leisure and health, among others. Without adequate services and

---

[100] STJ, REsp n°. 1.733.468/MG, 3ª Turma, Rel. Minister Nancy Andrighi, j. on 19/06/2018. The São Paulo State Court of Justice also takes the same view as the STJ and recognises inaccessibility on public transport as an unlawful act: TJSP, Appeal 1068320-23.2016.8.26.0100, 24th Chamber of Private Law. Rel. Walter Barone, j. on 31/07/2018: "PASSENGER TRANSPORT. Indemnity action for moral damage. Judgement upheld in part. Irresignation of the defendant. Partly justified. Plaintiff who needs a wheelchair to get around. Manoel Feio station, of which the plaintiff is a user, does not have a track crossing mechanism for wheelchair users. The plaintiff usually transfers in order to access an accessibility ramp at another station, but on the day of the events, she was unable to change trains due to a circulation problem on the railway network and, in order to leave the station, she was forced to leave her chair[100] STJ, REsp n°. 1.733.468/MG, 3ª Turma, Rel. Ministra Nancy Andrighi, j. em 19/06/2018. The São Paulo State Court of Justice also takes the same view as the STJ and recognises inaccessibility on public transport as an unlawful act: TJSP, Appeal 1068320-23.2016.8.26.0100, 24th Chamber of Private Law. Rel. Walter Barone, j. on 31/07/2018: "PASSENGER TRANSPORT. Indemnity action for moral damage. Judgement upheld in part. Irresignation of the defendant. Partly justified. Plaintiff who needs a wheelchair to get around. Manoel Feio station, of which the plaintiff is a user, does not have a track crossing mechanism for wheelchair users. The plaintiff usually changes trains in order to access an accessibility ramp at another station, but on the day of the events, he was unable to change trains due to a circulation problem on the railway network and, in order to leave the station, he was forced to leave his wheelchair behind.

equal opportunities with other individuals, people with disabilities are excluded from urban spaces and social interactions, which further aggravates the segregation that has historically been imposed on them. (8) The appellant, as a public service concessionaire and social actor, abruptly failed in its duty to promote the integration and inclusion of people with disabilities, going against the social and legal movement that culminated in the promulgation of the Convention and, domestically, in the drafting of the LBI. (9) As the judgement under appeal pointed out, there were successive failures in the provision of the service, such as the non-functioning lift to access the buses and the discriminatory treatment meted out to the user by the concessionaire's staff. The appellant's reluctance to provide the service to the respondent was such that it led to the unusual situation of the user "having to hide and ask someone else to give the signal, because the bus driver wouldn't stop if he saw him at the bus stop." 10. 10 In this scenario, moral damage, understood as an injury to the sphere of the individual's personality rights, stands out clearly. The physical and attitudinal barriers imposed by the appellant and its agents had repercussions on the defendant-plaintiff's subjective sphere, restricting his right to mobility. (11) There is no need to talk about reducing the quantum of compensation, estimated by the court of origin at R$25,000.00 (twenty-five thousand reais), given the seriousness of the attack on the defendant's dignity as a human being. 12) Special appeal known and not upheld, with an increase in the attorney's fees.

The Espírito Santo State Court of Justice has also recognised moral damage resulting from inaccessibility on public transport[101]

CIVIL APPEAL. MAIN AND ADHESIVE APPEAL. INDEMNITY ACTION FOR MORAL DAMAGE. STRICT LIABILITY. LICENCE HOLDER. URBAN PUBLIC TRANSPORT. PHYSICALLY DISABLED. LACK OF ACCESSIBILITY. DISRESPECT AND OFFENCE TO DIGNITY DURING BOARDING. OFF-BALANCE SHEET DAMAGE ESTABLISHED. QUANTUM OF COMPENSATION. INCREASE. INTEREST ON ARREARS. INITIAL TERM, CONTRACTUAL LIABILITY. CITATION. FEES. APPROPRIATE PERCENTAGE. APPEALS ACKNOWLEDGED AND PARTIALLY PROVIDED. 1 The preconditions for strict liability laid down in art. 37, § 6º , of the Constitution of the Republic, are the administrative event, the damage and the causal link between the administrative event and the damage. (2) In this case, the plaintiff, who is only nine years old, has a physical disability and uses a wheelchair, boarded the public transport of the defendant, a private legal entity providing a public service (permissionaire), which did not have accessibility devices, and whose driver, in addition to not helping the wheelchair-bound child to board (as did the fare collector), did not wait for him to finish, and drove off with the vehicle, leaving the plaintiff's younger sister and all her belongings, including the wheelchair, on the pavement. (3) The plaintiff's boarding behaviour was disrespectful and offensive to his dignity, which, in the circumstances described, goes beyond mere routine discomfort and constitutes damage to his extra-patrimonial sphere, especially since he is a person who, as well as being a child, is physically disabled, and whose State and society have the role of protecting and integrating. (4) As for the amount of compensation, taking into account the principles of proportionality and reasonableness, as well as the subjective and objective criteria pertinent to the case in question, in addition to the opinion of the Public Prosecutor's Office and case law in cases of difficulties caused for disabled people and wheelchair users to enter public transport, the amount arbitrated by the Court of origin should be increased to R$8,000.00. 5. interest for late payment in condemnation for moral damage flows from the date of the summons, in the case of contractual liability, as in the case of passenger transport. [9. appeal known and partially upheld to increase the compensation for moral damage to R$8,000.00 (eight thousand reais).

The São Paulo State Court of Justice has recognised the right to compensation for moral damage due to inaccessibility in a condominium[102] :

CIVIL LIABILITY. FALL OF DISABLED TENANT INSIDE GARAGE. ABSENCE OF HANDRAIL. NEGLIGENT CONDUCT OF THE CONDOMINIUM EVIDENCED. DELAY IN

---

[101] TJES, Appeal no. 048110018503, 2ª Civil Chamber, Substitute Rapporteur Delio Jose Rocha Sobrinho, j. on 12/12/2017.
[102] TJSP, Appeal 0168799-22.2008.8.26.0100, 26ª Chamber of Private Law King. Alfredo Attié, j. on 20/06/2018.

Another ruling by the São Paulo State Court of Justice demonstrates the possibility of recognising moral damage in its own right due to inaccessibility[103] :

> APPEAL - Appeal - "Indemnity action for moral damages" - Insurgency against the judgement upheld - Inadmissibility - Incontrovertible lack of adequate access for people with physical disabilities - Defendants had to access the appellant bank branch with a wheelchair Inadmissibility - Incontrovertible lack of adequate access for people with physical disabilities - Appellants had to access the appellant bank's branch with a wheelchair, going up and then down the vehicle access ramp, without any assistance from the appellant's employees - Evident failure to provide banking services - Moral damage "in re ipsa" characterised - Compensation duly set, in compliance with the principles of reasonableness and proportionality for the specific case - Attorney's fees well set, and which may be increased under the terms of article 85, § 11, of the CPC/2015 - Sentence upheld - Appeal dismissed.

The Statute for People with Disabilities further consolidated this understanding, which had already been built up, by addressing accessibility as a personality right.

Given the fundamental values guaranteed by accessibility, there is no doubt about the need for compensation for the moral damage caused by inaccessibility.

5.2. The person responsible for compensation.

Article 8º of Law 13.146/2015 establishes a general rule on the duty to promote the rights of people with disabilities, including accessibility:

> Art. 8º . It is the duty of the state, society and the family to ensure that people with disabilities, as a matter of priority, have their rights to life, health, sexuality, paternity and maternity, food, housing, education, vocational training, work, social security, habilitation and rehabilitation, transport, accessibility, culture, sport, tourism, leisure, information, communication, scientific and technological advances, dignity, respect, freedom, family and community coexistence, among others arising from the Federal Constitution, the Convention on the Rights of Persons with Disabilities and its Optional Protocol and the laws and other norms that guarantee their personal, social and economic well-being.

It can be seen from the normative wording that accessibility and all the other rights of people with disabilities or reduced mobility are the responsibility of society as a whole.

The violation of a legal duty characterises an illicit act and, as a rule, this causes damage to someone, generating a new legal duty to repair the damage. It is in this sense that the concept of civil liability arises, which is precisely this duty to repair damage caused by the breach of a legal duty. Thus, whenever you want to identify who is liable, you need to know who violated the pre-existing legal duty, since it is a successive duty[104] .

In order to contribute to this discussion, the attribution of responsibility can be systematised as follows, based

---

[103] TJSP, Appeal 1012210-18.2014.8.26.0506, 18ª Chamber of Private Law; King. Roque Antonio Mesquita de Oliveira, j. on 14/11/2017.
[104] CAVALIERI FILHO, Sérgio. *Civil Liability Programme,* ob. cit.

on art. 8° of the Statute for Persons with Disabilities:

RESPONSIBLE	SITUATION
Direct Public Administration Entities (Union, States, Federal District and Municipalities)	On public roads (streets, squares, motorways) and direct administration offices.
Indirect Public Administration Entities (Autarchies, Foundations, Public Companies, Mixed Economy Companies)	In their offices and spaces for which they are responsible.
Private individuals	In private property for collective use, such as shops, service establishments, condominiums, companies, *etc.*
Family	In domestic support, in the home, in the residence.

Anyone whose business is open to the public must adapt the physical space in which they work to ensure accessibility for people with disabilities[105] .

In order to establish civil liability, there are three essential prerequisites: 1) an unlawful act attributable to someone; 2) damage; and 3) a causal link[106] .

In order to insert these assumptions in the case of inaccessibility, it is possible to consider that the unlawful act is the failure to comply with accessibility standards, in other words, the omissive behaviour of a certain agent. The damage, in turn, is moral damage, an offence against the individual's personality. Finally, the causal link is the link between the causal event and the damage and will be verified when the lack of accessibility prevents or hinders the disabled individual from exercising a certain right[107] .

Article 56, §2 of the Statute, for example, states that the public authorities are responsible for approving, licensing or issuing certificates for executive architectural and urban projects and for temporary or permanent installations and equipment, and must certify that they comply with accessibility rules.

In turn, art. 58 establishes that construction companies and developers responsible for the design and construction of private multi-family buildings must comply with accessibility precepts, and must also ensure a minimum percentage of fully accessible units, with no additional charges being levied for their acquisition.

Thus, the person responsible for compensating moral damage resulting from inaccessibility must be identified in accordance with the rules that determine responsibility for promoting accessibility.

As an example, see the following judgement[108] :

> INTERLOCUTORY APPEAL IN THE PLAINTIFFS' APPEAL. INDEMNITY FOR MORAL DAMAGES. LACK OF ACCESS TO THE COMPANY'S SPECIAL TOILET BY AN EMPLOYEE WITH PARAPLEGIA. QUANTUM OF COMPENSATION REDUCED TO R$ 15,000.00 (FIFTEEN THOUSAND REAIS). CRITERIA OF REASONABLENESS AND

---

[105] As an example, the Court of Justice of the State of Espírito Santo recognised this duty of those who carry out activities aimed at the public and had to pay compensation for the inaccessibility of their physical space: "CIVIL APPEAL. PHYSICALLY DISABLED. INACCESSIBILITY. DUTY TO INDEMNIFY. UNDUE DENIAL OF CREDIT. EXCLUSIVE FAULT OF THE CONSUMER NOT DEMONSTRATED. MORAL DAMAGE IN RE IPSA. APPEAL DISMISSED. 1 With regard to the condemnation of the appellant in relation to the accessibility of the appellee's bank branch, the judgement does not deserve to be retouched, since the responsibility lies with everyone, as expressly provided for in the Federal Constitution and the Governing Legislation. 2 It is the responsibility, above all, of public entities or those that carry out activities of a public nature to provide ample and unrestricted possibility for the disabled person to feel fully integrated and to be able to carry out any activity. (3) The consumer's exclusive fault is unfounded, insofar as, in the case in question, the consumer appealed against took steps to make the payments due, and it is absolutely unacceptable to impute any responsibility to him for subsequently having his name blacklisted as a result of the alleged non-payment. 4 . As for the failure to prove moral damage, it should be emphasised that the case in question is enshrined in case law as moral damage in re ipsa, i.e. which does not require proof of actual damage. 5. appeal known and dismissed". (TJES, Appeal no. 064160020257, Iª Civil Chamber, King. Ewerton Schwab Pinto Júnior, j. on 24/10/2017).
[106] NORONHA, Fernando. *Law of Obligations*. 3ª ed. São Paulo: Saraiva, 2010, p. 492.
[107] NORONHA, Fernando. *Law of Obligations*, ob. cit., p. 499.
[108] TST, ARR 817-33.2011.5.15.0003,2ª Turma, Rei. Min. José Roberto Freire Pimenta, j. on 02/09/2015.

Although the above-mentioned ruling was handed down by the Superior Labour Court, it deals with moral damage resulting from non-compliance with accessibility standards: the employer, Carrefour Comércio e Indústria Ltda., was ordered to pay compensation for moral damage to a disabled employee who did not have access to an accessible toilet.

The reasoning used by the court of first instance for the conviction is based on non-compliance with the accessibility standards laid down in Law No. 10.098/2000, stating the following:

> The company's premises should have the legal minimum of accessibility for customers, as well as for its disabled employees. In this respect, having hired a disabled person as an employee, the defendant should have provided accessible and adequate means to improve the plaintiff's living conditions. However, from the evidence in the case file, I can see that there was no due respect for the right to accessibility for people with physical disabilities, especially the plaintiff.

This understanding was upheld by the Regional Labour Court, but with a reduction in the *amount of* compensation, as it was considered exorbitant, which was upheld by the Superior Labour Court.

Finally, it should be noted that the employer was held liable precisely because it was responsible for providing a minimum number of accessible toilets under the terms of Law 10.098/2000.

It is therefore possible to speak of the responsibility of those who fail to fulfil their obligation to guarantee accessibility for people with disabilities, since such an omission jeopardises the exercise of many fundamental rights of these people who need special attention to fully exercise their dignity.

5.3. Specific protection of the right to accessibility

Although pecuniary compensation for off-balance sheet damage is important for protecting the right to accessibility, there are other forms of protection that are also essential for guaranteeing broad protection for personality rights.

As well as providing for the possibility of an award of a pecuniary sum for damage resulting from inaccessibility, the legal system also offers remedies capable of preventing the occurrence, continuation or repetition of the offending offence against the rights of people with disabilities.

Alongside compensatory protection for off-balance sheet damage, injunctions and cessation remedies must also be used to ensure that the right to accessibility is fully protected. Injunctions are used to prevent unlawful behaviour by imposing duties to do or not to do, i.e. abstention. On the other hand, once a transgression has occurred, injunctive relief is capable of enabling the right to accessibility to be exercised, preventing the perpetuation or repetition of the offence, through the imposition of duties to do.

In fact, inaccessibility can constitute unlawful conduct that lasts over time and doesn't end with just one act, such as the impossibility of access to certain public buildings, commercial establishments, residential condominiums, parking spaces, as well as inaccessibility to certain products and services, due to the lack of communication in *Braille* and Libras, which prevents people with visual or hearing disabilities from hiring, *etc.*

In these cases, injunctive relief is appropriate, which, by enabling the realisation of the right to accessibility, prevents the continuation or reiteration of the unlawful act, by imposing obligations to do things, such as: carrying out works, building ramps, installing lifts and stairlifts, allocating exclusive parking spaces for people with disabilities, using *Braille* and Libras in contracts, *etc.* These measures, embodied in obligations to do, not only guarantee the right to accessibility, but also cease the continuation of the unlawful act that is perpetuated over time, which characterises the provision of injunctive relief.

As the right to accessibility has an off-balance sheet nature[109] , i.e. it cannot be measured in money, it can be said that the holder of the violated right will never be fully compensated simply by being awarded a monetary sum, as the offence affects goods, attributes and values that cannot be economically assessed, thus causing moral damage that cannot be compensated with money alone.

Anderson Schreiber warns: "While it is true that, in the field of property damage, the award of compensation in money restores the victim to their previous situation by restoring their assets, this is clearly not the case in relation to moral damage."[110] .

In the procedural sphere, therefore, the full protection of personality rights depends on effective access to justice and the suitability of the judicial remedy to the material right at stake[111] . Access to justice can no longer be seen as a mere formal guarantee of provocation and access to the judiciary, but as a guarantee of access to the "just legal order"[112] , with the provision of efficient, effective and adequate protection for the substantive right[113] .

The process, therefore, must be capable of guaranteeing the full protection of personality rights, by means of appropriate techniques for their satisfaction, taking into account their off-balance sheet nature[114] .

Luiz Guilherme Marinoni emphasises that judicial protection must be effective and adequate to protect the material right being pursued[115] .

> The right to judicial protection, which stems from the very existence of the substantive right and the prohibition on its private realisation, is not just the right to go to the courts, but the right to use the appropriate technique so that the substantive right can be effectively protected. The right to judicial protection, in this sense, is the right to the procedural technique (for example, judgement and executive means) capable of enabling the effective protection of the substantive right.

Along the same lines, José Roberto dos Santos Bedaque emphasises the meaning that should be given to the term "judicial protection", relating it to the need to protect the material right effectively and adequately[116] .

> Jurisdictional protection should therefore be understood as the effective protection of rights or situations through the process. It is a view of procedural law that emphasises the outcome of the

---

[109] Cristiano Chaves de Farias and Nelson Rosenvald write about the off-balance-sheet nature of personality rights and the possibility of pecuniary compensation for moral damage resulting from their violation: "Off-balance-sheet nature consists of the impossibility of economic appreciation of personality rights, even though any injury may produce monetary consequences (in this case, compensation for off-balance-sheet damage, commonly referred to as moral damage). The issue requires clarification. It is certain and uncontroversial that honour, privacy and other personal legal assets of a person cannot be valued in monetary terms. They are existential values and therefore not susceptible to monetary measurement, to a patrimonial value. However, once there has been a violation of these personality values, regardless of whether it causes material damage, there is the possibility of compensation for the moral damage characterised, as a way of compensating the damage imposed on the victim [...] (FARIAS, Cristiano Chaves de; ROSENVALD, Nelson. *Civil Law Course. General Part and LINDB*. Vol. 1. 15ª ed. Salvador: Juspodivm, 2017, p. 190-191). In the same vein, Gustavo Tepedino states: "The off-balance sheet nature of these rights would consist of the fact that they are not susceptible to economic evaluation, even if their injury generates economic repercussions" (TEPEDINO, Gustavo. *Temas de Direito Civil*. 4th ed. Rio de Janeiro: Renovar, 2008, p. 36).

[110] SCHREIBER, Anderson. *Civil law and the constitution*. São Paulo: Atlas, 2013, p. 207.

[111] HIBNER, Davi Amaral. *The protection of personality rights in the 2015 Code of Civil Procedure*. Master's dissertation. Postgraduate Law Programme. Federal University of Espírito Santo. Supervisor: Prof Dr Gilberto Fachetti Silvestre. Vitória, 2018-2019, Chap. 4.

[112] WATANABE, Kazuo. Preliminary injunctions and specific injunctions for obligations to do and not to do. In: TEIXEIRA, Sálvio de Figueiredo (coord.). *Reforma do Código de Processo Civil*. São Paulo: Saraiva, 2006, p. 20.

[113] MARINONI, Luiz Guilherme. *Tort remedies: injunctions and removal*. São Paulo: Revista dos Tribunais, 2015, p. 61.

[114] HIBNER, Davi Amaral. *The protection of personality rights in the 2015 Code of Civil Procedure*, ob. cit.

[115] MARINONI, Luiz Guilherme. *Injunctions and remedies against unlawful acts*, ob. cit.

[116] BEDAQUE, José Roberto dos Santos. *Law and Process: the influence of substantive law on process*. 6ª ed. São Paulo: Malheiros, 2011, p. 37.

> process as a factor in guaranteeing the material right. [...] The procedural technique at the service of its result. Adequate protection of a substantive right has as its content the guarantee of protection of that right. This guarantee, when ensured by the court, constitutes judicial protection. [...] Jurisdictional protection thus has the meaning of protecting a right or a legal situation through the courts.

It is in this sense that, taking into account the result that the process provides to the parties in terms of substantive law, judicial protection can be classified as specific or generic (or for the pecuniary equivalent)[117]
.

Andrea Proto Pisani succinctly defines the concept of specific protection: "Tutela specifica: con questa espressione si indica quella tutela diretta a fare conseguire al titolare del diritto quelle stesse utilità garantitegli dalla legge (o dal contratto) e non utilità equivalente"[118] .

In a similar vein, José Carlos Barbosa Moreira states that specific protection means "the set of remedies and measures aimed at providing the person for whose benefit the obligation was established [...] with the precise practical result attainable through fulfilment, i.e. the *non-infringement* of the right or interest being protected"[119] .

In the context of personality rights, including the right to accessibility, "protection will be specific if it is capable of preventing damage to personality rights, ensuring their safety, or when, in the event of damage, it is capable of restoring the violated legal asset and/or guaranteeing the exercise of the offended right"[120] .

On the other hand, "the generic remedy corresponds to the losses and damages resulting from the failure to fulfil the specific remedy", as Cassio Scarpinella Bueno explains[121] . In other words, "in the equivalent remedy, the rightful party is not given exactly the good of life that was taken from them, but rather an equivalent in money", as Fredie Didier Jr, Leonardo Carneiro da Cunha, Paula Samo Braga and Rafael Alexandria de Oliveira state[122] .

Adopting the conceptual definitions drawn up by the legal literature, it can be said that, in the protection of the right to accessibility, injunctive relief is a specific form of protection, since it is capable of preventing the practice of the offence and, consequently, the extra-patrimonial damage resulting from inaccessibility.

For example, in the event of the construction of a building for the operation of commercial activities in which there are no means of access for people with disabilities, it is possible to grant injunctive relief to prevent the commencement of trade without complying with accessibility standards, thus avoiding the violation of the rights of people with disabilities. In this case, injunctive relief can consist of imposing duties *(i)* not to do anything, i.e. to abstain (not to start activities), and *(ii)* to do something (to carry out works to ensure accessibility). The fulfilment of both duties can be ensured by setting a pecuniary fine, under the terms of art. 536, § I° , of the CPC.

It is also possible to grant injunctive relief, in the form of cessation, to protect the right to accessibility, by imposing obligations to do something, with the aim of preventing the reiteration or continuation of the illegal act and guaranteeing the exercise of the right to accessibility. For example, injunctive relief can be granted to oblige the Public Administration to carry out works that allow access and mobility for people on public roads, with *astreintes* set to ensure compliance with the obligation to do so. In this case, injunctive relief is capable

---

[117] DIDIER JR., Fredie; CUNHA, Leonardo Carneiro da; BRAGA, Paula Samo; OLIVEIRA, Rafael Alexandria de. *Civil Procedural Law Course. Execution.* Vol. 5. 7ª ed. Salvador: Juspodivm, 2017, p. 567-568; BUENO, Cassio Scarpinella. *Systematised course of civil procedural law: general theory of civil procedural law and general part of the Code of Civil Procedure.* Vol. 1. 9ª ed. São Paulo, Saraiva, 2018, p. 366-369.

[118] PISANI, Andrea Proto. *Lezioni di diritto proceduale civile.* 5ª ed. Napoli: Jovene Editora, 2006, pp. 746 and 748.

[119] BARBOSA MOREIRA, José Carlos. Specific protection of the creditor in negative obligations. *Brazilian Journal of Procedural Law.* Rio de Janeiro, Vol. 20, p. 63, 1979.

[120] HIBNER, Davi Amaral. *The protection of personality rights in the 2015 Code of Civil Procedure,* ob. cit.

[121] BUENO, Cassio Scarpinella. *Systematised course in civil procedural law...,* ob. cit.

[122] DIDIER JR., Fredie; CUNHA, Leonardo Carneiro da; BRAGA, Paula Samo; OLIVEIRA, Rafael Alexandria de. *Course in Civil Procedural Law,* ob. cit.

of preventing the perpetuation or repetition of the unlawful act, as well as making it possible to enjoy the right to accessibility, by imposing an obligation to do something, consisting of carrying out works that comply with the technical standards for accessibility and urban mobility.

In this regard, the Superior Court of Justice upheld a judgement that ordered the Municipality of São Paulo to carry out work to adapt and lower pavements to the standards of NBR 9050 - ABNT, in order to ensure full accessibility for people with disabilities[123] :

> 1. This is a Public Civil Action filed by the Public Prosecutor's Office of the State of São Paulo against Santos City Hall, seeking to order the defendant to comply with the obligation to make the pavements in the Emba neighbourhood conform to the standards of NBR 9050 - ABNT, in order to guarantee full accessibility for people with disabilities. 2. °The trial judge partially upheld the action, in order to order the municipality to lower the curbs at all the intersections of the twenty public roads chosen by the administration to be paved in the so-called "Embaré street resurfacing programme", adopting the dictates of NBR 9050 - ABNT, within 6 months, under penalty of a daily fine of R$ 1,000.00. 3. (3) The lower court thus stated: "In reality, all that is sought in this action is for the streets already chosen and remodelled by the Municipality to have their pavements lowered for the circulation of the disabled, in accordance with the standards of NBR 9050, by express determination of the law, compliance with which is not within the discretion of the administrator. Therefore, in the case at hand, the solution adopted by the sentencing magistrate was correct, and there was no undue intrusion by the Judiciary." (fl. 176, emphasis added). 4. special appeal not upheld.

In the same vein, the São Paulo Court of Justice ordered the Municipality of Santos to carry out works to ensure accessibility for people with disabilities to a waterway terminal[124] :

> Appeal. Public Civil Action. Claim by the MPSP to order the Municipality of Santos to carry out accessibility works for people with disabilities around the Santos - Vicente de Carvalho waterway terminal. Judgement upheld, imposing a daily fine for non-compliance. Reversed only with regard to the fine, but upheld on the merits. Curtailment of defence. No defence. Sufficient documentation in the case file to investigate the incompleteness of the accessibility works and their implementation in breach of technical standards. Procedural interest. Present. Numerous attempts at amicable settlement by the MPSP, which were not taken up by the Municipality. Continence. Non-occurrence. Actions that have different objectives. Accessibility for people with disabilities to public buildings and areas is a constitutional guarantee, part of the existential minimum for a dignified life. The Constitution of the Republic determines that public places must be adapted to ensure accessibility for people with disabilities. Federal Law No. 10.098/00, which determines the application of ABNT technical standards to accessibility reforms. The Judiciary may, exceptionally, order the Administration to realise essential constitutional rights without this meaning a violation of the separation of powers. The principle of the reserve of the possible cannot be opposed to the existential minimum. STJ and STF precedents. Daily fine and deadline for compliance. Reform to reduce the fine and the deadline, so that there is no new punishment for society. Sentence reformed, only with regard to the fine for non-compliance. Appeal partially upheld.

---

[123] STJ, REsp. n° 1320356/SP, King. Justice Herman Benjamin, Second Panel, judged on 25/10/2016.

[124] TJSP, Appeal and Necessary Remand No. 1029477-58.2016.8.26.0562, Rapporteur Marcelo Semer, 10ª Chamber of Public Law, judged on 18/06/2018. In the same vein: "Public Civil Action - Adaptation of a public building for accessibility for people with disabilities or reduced mobility - Art. 227, §2 and 244 of the Federal Constitution - State Law No. 11.263/02 which established the conditions and a deadline of five years from its entry into force for the implementation of the necessary architectural modifications - Exhausted deadline - Omission by the Public Authority characterised - No violation of the principle of separation of powers and administrative discretion - Appeal dismissed, in this part. Daily fine - Adequate amount, only limitation of the maximum amount is appropriate - Time limit of 120 days to fulfil the obligation compatible with the size of the work and the delay of the Public Authority - Appeal partially upheld, in this part. Appeal by the State of São Paulo upheld in part". (TJSP, Appeal No. 1015360-45.2015.8.26.0482, Rapporteur Luciana Bresciani, 2ª Chamber of Public Law, judged on 09/04/2018).

In order to guarantee broad protection for the right to accessibility, it is even possible to impose obligations not only on the government, but also on private individuals, such as companies that supply products and services. In this regard, the Superior Court of Justice upheld a ruling by the Rio de Janeiro Court of Justice, which, based on the International Convention on the Rights of Persons with Disabilities and the Consumer Defence Code, ordered a financial institution to produce contracts and bank statements in *Braille,* as well as to pay compensation for collective extra-patrimonial damage, in order to protect the right to information of visually impaired people[125] :

> 2. Even if there wasn't, as in fact there is, a specific legal protection system for people with disabilities (Laws No. 4.169/62, 10.048/2000, 10.098/2000 and Decree No. 6.949/2009), the obligation to use the braille method in banking contracts with people with visual impairments is based, in addition to the consumer legislation applicable *in total*, on the principle of the Dignity of the Human Person. 2.1 The International Convention on the Rights of Persons with Disabilities imposes on signatory states the obligation to ensure the full and equal enjoyment of all human rights and fundamental freedoms by persons with disabilities, granting them materially equal treatment (differentiated in proportion to their inequality) and therefore non-discriminatory, physical accessibility and communication and information, social inclusion, autonomy and independence (as far as possible, of course), and freedom to make their own choices, all to enable the realisation of the greater principle of the Dignity of the Human Person. 2.2 Using the definitions provided by the Treaty, it is safe to say that the failure to use the Braille method throughout the banking relationship with a visually impaired person (a measure which, admittedly, does not impose a disproportionate burden on the financial institution), preventing them from exercising their basic consumer rights on an equal footing with other people and exacerbating the inherent difficulty of accessing related information, constitutes, at the same time, intolerable discrimination on the grounds of disability and non-compliance with the desired "reasonable accommodation". 2.3 The adoption of the Braille method in banking agreements with visually impaired people is also unquestionably based on consumer legislation, which states that it is a basic consumer right to be provided with sufficiently adequate and clear information about the product or service offered, a duty that must be observed not only when the agreement is signed, but also throughout the contract. In the case of visually impaired consumers, this right can only be fully realised in a bank contract by using the Braille method, which facilitates and even enables them to fully understand and reflect on the contractual clauses submitted to them, especially those which imply limitations on their rights, as well as the monthly statements showing the services provided, fees charged, etc. [...] 3. [The jurisprudence of the Superior Court of Justice has favoured the position that it is possible, in theory, to configure collective extra-patrimonial damage, whenever the injury or threat of injury carried out by the defendant greatly affects the fundamental values and interests of the group, and it therefore seems unreasonable to deny this community compensation for its degraded immaterial heritage. 3.1 In this case, the defendant financial institution's reluctance to use the Braille method in bank contracts with visually impaired people, giving them manifestly discriminatory treatment, has the effect of greatly exacerbating the inherent difficulties of access to communication and essential information for individuals in this peculiar condition, the practice of which, in addition to constituting significant contractual abuse, is a real affront to the dignity of the group itself, collectively considered. [The setting of astreintes, whether for a tiny or exorbitant amount, as is the case here, inevitably has the same consequences: Favouring the debtor's recalcitrant behaviour in complying with court decisions, as well as encouraging the use of appeals to this Superior Court, precisely to measure the appropriate amount. For this reason, the ordinary courts, with a view to the consequentialism of their decisions, must weigh up when defining the astreintes. (6) The judgement handed down in this class action aimed at protecting collective rights stricto sensu - considering their indivisibility - produces effects in relation to all visually impaired consumers who litigate or will litigate with the defendant financial institution throughout the national territory. Panel precedent. 7. special appeal partially granted.

In the Espírito Santo Court of Justice, there is a judgement in which a concessionaire of public road transport services was ordered to adapt its fleet of vehicles to accessibility standards, being obliged to install platform lifts or access ramps on the buses that carry out the public urban transport of the population of the Municipality

---

[125] STJ, REsp. n° 1315822/RJ, King. Minister Marco Aurélio Belizze, Third Chamber, judged on 24/03/2015.

of Marataízes, which characterises the provision of injunctive relief, aimed at preventing the perpetuation and reiteration of the illicit act, making effective the right to mobility[126] :

> 5. Merits: In reality, the judge of first instance was attentive to the strict terms of the cause of action and the request, having only partially accepted the latter because he considered that the provision of 1/3 (one third) of the fleet of Viação Sudeste LTDA used in urban transport in the municipality of Marataízes in accordance with the aforementioned technical guidelines, or at least 01 (one) adapted bus for each of the urban lines operated by it, is sufficient to guarantee accessibility for people with disabilities to public transport. 6 Merits: The documentary evidence produced in the case file, in particular the timetable provided by the DER-ES and the letter from the Marataízes Municipal Transport Secretary prove that it is only the appellant that carries out municipal urban public transport and that the buses serving the urban area are equipped with turnstiles. 7 Merits: The existence of a fare control device means that the appellant's buses cannot be characterised as road buses, in accordance with NBR 15320:2005 of the European Commission.
> ABNT, which indicates that the economic activity of Viação Sudeste Ltda. is not restricted to intercity road transport. 8. merits: It should be added that the National Institute of Metrology, Standardisation and Industrial Quality INMETRO, by means of Ordinance No. 357 of 13 September 2010, established the mandatory installation of elevating platforms or access ramps, in accordance with the requirements of NBR 15646, including for road buses, and information provided by the appellant's manager that the vehicles travelling in the municipality of Marataízes do not meet these requirements has been attached to the case file. Therefore, the guidelines of NBR 14022 and NBR 15646 are fully applicable to the appellant's vehicles that carry out urban public transport in the municipality of Marataízes. [Merits: The fine set in the judgement is unreasonable, and it is sufficient and compatible with the obligation to do in question for the astreintes to be arbitrated at the daily level of R$ 1,000.00 (one thousand reais) and limited to the amount of R$ 100,000.00 (one hundred thousand reais), without prejudice to new grounds that may influence the enforcement phase of the judgement.

In lawsuits between private individuals, it is also possible to grant injunctions aimed at protecting the right to accessibility. In a claim brought by a disabled person against the condominium in which she lives, the São Paulo Court of Justice granted injunctive relief and compensatory relief, ordering the condominium to carry out works to ensure accessibility and to pay "compensation" for the non-pecuniary damage resulting from inaccessibility[127] :

> The Statute for People with Disabilities stipulates that accessibility rules apply to existing buildings - access ramp, glass door, lowering of intercoms, parking spaces; - Moral damage established: negligence on the part of the liquidator and the condominium towards the plaintiffs, since even after requests for help and internal changes, the measures were not carried out, in addition to the denial of help from employees; - Extension of the deadline for carrying out the works in the condominium garage.

As can be seen from some of the judgements cited, injunctive relief was combined with compensatory relief for off-balance sheet damage. As has been pointed out, damage to personality rights, including the right to

---

[126] TJES, Class: Appeal No. 069150044647, Rapporteur Fernando Estevam Bravin Ruy, Second Civil Chamber, judged on 07/11/2017.

[127] TJSP, Appeal No. 1021847-76.2016.8.26.0003, Rapporteur Maria Lúcia Pizzotti, 30ª Chamber of Private Law, judged on 28/02/2018. In another judgement, the São Paulo Court of Justice granted injunctive relief to a disabled person, ordering the condominium with shared parking spaces to allow the plaintiff to exclusively use a parking space considered to be easily accessible: "Despite the lack of a specific rule imposing the reservation of parking spaces in residential or private condominiums for the disabled, the different condition of the plaintiff-condominium owner must be respected in relation to the other residents who, because they do not suffer from physical movement restrictions, will enjoy the other existing parking spaces" (TJSP, Appeal No. 1013283-02.2016.8.26.0006, Rapporteur Renato Sartorelli, 26ª Chamber of Private Law, judged on 10/04/2018).

accessibility, generates moral damage *in re ipsa*. In other words, the violation of personality rights will always cause off-balance sheet damage.

In the event of damage to the right to accessibility, it is possible to combine injunctive relief with compensatory relief through the payment of money.

Injunctive relief, with the imposition of a requirement to do something, makes it possible to exercise the right to accessibility and, consequently, prevents the perpetuation (and reiteration) of the offence, while compensatory relief acts as an indemnity for the off-balance sheet damage resulting from inaccessibility.

Thus, in the event of damage to the right to accessibility, the remedy can be specific with a combination of injunctive-cessory and compensatory-remedial remedies, since, in addition to compensating for the off-balance sheet damage resulting from the illegal act, it is necessary to make the right to accessibility effective/enforceable, thereby preventing the continuation and repetition of the illegal act.

CHAPTER 6

CONCLUSION

The legislative and social treatment of people with disabilities in Brazil and around the world has undergone a significant transformation. Today, people with disabilities are no longer seen as incapable, or as people who simply have their own limitations and are exclusively analysed using medical concepts.

Disabilities have come to be seen as difficulties imposed by the environment in which the person lives. In this sense, it is no longer appropriate to exclude people with disabilities from the social environment. On the contrary, more and more efforts are being made to adapt the environment to the person, so that they can live a life of full inclusion and social participation.

In this context, accessibility emerges as an essential right for human personality, since it allows for this longed-for inclusion and is also an indispensable element for the realisation of equality and dignity for people with disabilities.

Accessibility can be seen as the realisation of the idea of adapting the environment to the person, so that, regardless of any physical or mental specificity, everyone has access to public and private goods for collective use, as well as to information and full public and political participation. Accessibility therefore allows people with disabilities or reduced mobility to exercise their citizenship.

Law 13.146/2015 gave accessibility the *status of* a personality right. As a result, violating the right to accessibility generates moral damage, i.e. it causes extra-patrimonial harm to the person whose right has been damaged.

Compensation for moral damages resulting from inaccessibility should occur whenever access or the exercise of a certain right is hindered or prevented due to non-compliance with accessibility standards, which in itself already constitutes moral damage.

Alongside the compensatory protection of off-balance sheet damages, injunctive relief is important in protecting the right to accessibility. By imposing duties to do, it is possible to realise the exercise of this right, thus preventing the perpetuation or reiteration of the illicit act of inaccessibility.

Finally, it is known that in Brazil there is still a long way to go to fully realise accessibility and all the ideals sought by the Statute for People with Disabilities. But it is possible to glimpse major advances in these areas, which leads us to believe that in the future it will be possible to live in a society where people with disabilities do not face the difficulties of social inclusion that are still experienced today.

BIBLIOGRAPHICAL REFERENCES

AMARAL, Francisco. *Civil law: introduction.* 8ª ed. Rio de Janeiro: Renovar, 2014.

ARAÚJO, Luiz Alberto David; COSTA FILHO, Waldir Macieira da. The statute for people with disabilities - EPCD (Law no. 13.146, of 06.07.2015): some new features. In: *Revista dos Tribunais,* vol. 962, pp. 65-80, Dec/2015.

ARAÚJO, Luiz Alberto David; MAIA, Maurício. Constitutional urban environment and compliance with accessibility rules. In: *Revista de Direito Ambiental,* vol. 79, pp. 431-448, jul-set/2015.

ARAÚJO, Luiz Alberto David; MAIA, Maurício. The city, the constitutional duty of social inclusion and accessibility. In: *Revista de Direito da Cidade,* vol. 08, n° 1. Rio de Janeiro, 2016, pp.225-244.

ARENHART, Sérgio Cruz. *Injunctions against private life.* São Paulo: Revista dos Tribunais, 2000.

BRAZILIAN ASSOCIATION OF TECHNICAL STANDARDS. NBR 9050: Accessibility to buildings, furniture, spaces and urban equipment. 2015. Available at: <http://www.aedesenho.com.br/informativo/abnt-nbr-9050-2015-norma-acessibilidade- free/>. Accessed on: 13 June 2015

AZEVEDO, Antonio Junqueira de. Legal characterisation of the dignity of the human person. In: *Quarterly Journal of Civil Law,* vol. 09. Rio de Janeiro: Padma, Jan/Mar 2002, pp. 03-23.

BARBOSA MOREIRA, José Carlos. Specific protection of the creditor in negative obligations. In: *Brazilian Journal of Procedural Law*. Rio de Janeiro, Vol. 20, p. 63, 1979.

BARBOZA, Heloisa Helena; ALMEIDA JÚNIOR, Vitor de Azevedo. Recognition and inclusion of people with disabilities. In: *Brazilian Journal of Civil Law*. Belo Horizonte, vol. 13, p. 17-37, 2017.

BEDAQUE, José Roberto dos Santos. *Law and Process*. Influence of material law on process. 6ª ed. São Paulo: Malheiros, 2006.

BENTES, Hilda Helena Soares. Hephaestus able: from myth to the rights of people with disabilities. In: *Revista Jurídica da Presidência Brasília*, v. 19, n. 118, Jun./Sept. 2017, pp. 352-376.

BUENO, Cassio Scarpinella. *Systematised course of civil procedural law: general theory of civil procedural law and general part of the Code of Civil Procedure*. Vol. 1. 9ª ed. São Paulo, Saraiva, 2018.

CAVALIERI FILHO, Sérgio. *Civil liability programme*. 1 Iª ed. São Paulo: Atlas, 2014.

DIDIER JR., Fredie; CUNHA, Leonardo Carneiro da; BRAGA, Paula Samo; and OLIVEIRA, Rafael Alexandria de. *Civil Procedural Law Course. Execution*. Vol. 5. 7ª ed. Salvador: JusPodvim, 2017.

DIDIER JR., Fredie. *Course in Civil Procedural Law*. Vol. 1. 18ª ed. Salvador: JusPodvim, 2016.

DIDIER JR., Fredie; BRAGA, Paula Samo; and OLIVEIRA, Rafael Alexandria de. *Civil Procedural Law Course*. Theory of Evidence, Evidentiary Law, Decision, Precedent, Judgement and Provisional Guardianship. Vol. 2. 1 Iª ed. Salvador: JusPodvim, 2016.

FARIAS, Cristiano Chaves de; ROSENVALD, Nelson. *Civil Law Course*. General Part and LINDB. Vol. 1. 15ª ed. Salvador: JusPodivm, 2017.

;. *Civil Law: General Theory*. 6ª ed. Rio de Janeiro: Lumen Juris, 2007.

FELICETTI, Suelen Aparecida; BERNARDINE, Angelita Gralak; CARTELI, Zulméia; SANTOS, Sandro Aparecido dos. Accessibility, orientation and mobility: a case study from the point of view of people who are blind or have low vision. In: *Divers@ Interdisciplinary Electronic Journal*. Matinhos, v. 9, n. 1, p. 39-51, jan./dez. 2016.

FERNANDES, Alexandre Cortez. *Civil Law. Introduction: people and property*. Caxias do Sul: EDUCS, 2012.

FERRAZ, Carolina Valença; LEITE, Glauber Salomão. Brazilian inclusion law and the "new" concept of disability: will it now "catch on"? Available at: <http://justificando.cartacapital.com.br/2015/08/20/lei-brasileira-de-inclusao-e-o-novo- conceito-de-deficiencia-sera-que-agora-vai-pegar/>. Accessed on: 13 June 2017.

FORNASIER, Mateus de Oliveira; LEITE, Flavia Piva Almeida. Fundamental rights to accessibility and urban mobility for people with disabilities: a systemic-autopoietic approach. In: *Revista de Direito da Cidade,* vol. 08, n° 3, 2016, pp. 908-933.

GABRILLI, Mara. Accessibility is much more than building a ramp. In: *Pandora Brasil Magazine,* No. 26, January 2011.

GAETANO, Stea. The civil protection of personal rights. In: *Rivista Telemática Diritto&Diritti. Published also in Rivista Giurisprudenziale,* 1, 2001.

HIBNER, Davi Amaral. *The protection of personality rights in the 2015 Code of Civil Procedure*. Master's dissertation. Postgraduate Law Programme. Federal University of Espírito Santo. Supervisor: Prof Dr Gilberto Fachetti Silvestre. Vitória, 2018-2019.

JAQUES, Karina. *Fundamental right to accessibility*. Available at: <http://webcache.googleusercontent.com/search?q=cache:nIsGyUIvEAMJ:www.stf.jus.br/rep ositorio/cms/portalTvJustica/portalTvJusticaNoticia/anexo/KARINA_JAQUES.doc+&cd=3& hl=en&ct=clnk&gl=br>. Accessed on: 19 Apr. 2017.

KANT, Immanuel. *Rationale for the Metaphysics of Manners*. São Paulo: Martin Claret, 2002.

LIMA, Maria Macena de Lima; VIEIRA, Marcelo de Mello; SILVA, Beatriz de Almeida Borges e. Reflexões sobre as pessoas com deficiência e sobre os impactos da Lei n° 13.146/2015 no estudo dos planos do negócio jurídico. In: *Brazilian Journal of Civil Law*. Belo Horizonte, vol. 14, p. 17-39, Oct./Dec. 2017.

MARINONI, Luiz Guilherme. *Procedural technique and the protection of rights*. 5ª ed. São Paulo: Brazil, 2018.

. Protection against unlawful behaviour (art. 497, sole paragraph, of the CPC/2015). In: *Revista de Processo*. São Paulo. Vol. 245. p. 313-329. Jul./2015.

. *Tort remedies: injunctions and injunctive relief*. São Paulo: Revista dos Tribunais, 2015.

. *Specific protection*. 2ª ed. São Paulo: RT, 2001.

. Individual and collective *injunctions*. 5ª ed. São Paulo: RT, 2012.

MARINONI, Luiz Guilherme; ARENHART, Sérgio Cruz; MITIDIERO, Daniel. *New Course in Civil Procedure'*. Theory of Civil Procedure. Vol. 1. São Paulo: Revista dos Tribunais, 2015.

;;. *New Course in Civil Procedure'*. Protection of rights through common procedure. Vol. 2. São Paulo: Revista dos Tribunais, 2015.

MENEZES, Joyceane Bezerra de; MENEZES, Herika Janaynna Bezerra de; MENEZES, Abraão Bezerra de. The approach to disability in the face of the expansion of human rights. In: *Revista de Direitos e Garantias Fundamentais*, 17(2), pp. 551-572, 2016.

MORAES, Celina Maria Bodin de. *Na medida da pessoa humana*. Studies in civil and constitutional law. Rio de Janeiro: Renovar, 2010.

. *Damage to the Human Person*. Rio de Janeiro: Renovar, 2013.

NERY, Rosa Maria de Andrade. Distinction between "personality" and "general right of personality": a discipline of its own. *Essential Doctrines of Constitutional Law*. São Paulo: Revista dos Tribunais, vol. 8. p. 473-478. Aug./2015.

NISHIYAMA, Adolfo Mamoru; TEIXEIRA, Carla Noura. The historical evolution of the protection of people with disabilities in Brazilian constitutions: current normative instruments for their realisation. In: *Revista de Direito Privado*, Vol. 68, p. 225-240, Aug/2016.

NORONHA, Fernando. *Law of obligations*. 3ª ed. São Paulo: Saraiva, 2010.

. *Law of obligations*. 4ª . ed. São Paulo: Saraiva, 2013.

PEREIRA, R. V.; LELIS, H. R. Equality and Human Dignity of People with Disabilities: Reflections of the New Inclusion Law-Law no. 13.146/2015-In the Health Sector. In: *Revista Brasileira de Direitos e Garantias Fundamentais*, 2(1), pp. 19-35, 2016.

PONTES DE MIRANDA, Francisco Cavalcanti. *Treatise on Private Law*. Special Part. Volume VIL Personality rights. Family law. São Paulo: RT, 2012.

. *Private Law Treatise*. Special Part. Volume LIII. Rights of Obligation. São Paulo: RT, 2012.

. *Private Law Treatise*. Special Part. Volume LIII. Rights of Obligation. São Paulo: Revista dos Tribunais, 2012.

SCHREIBER, Anderson. *Civil Law and the Constitution*. São Paulo: Atlas, 2013.

. *Personality rights*. 3ª Ed. São Paulo: Atlas, 2014.

. *New paradigms of civil liability:* from the erosion of reparation filters to the dilution of damages. 6ª ed. São Paulo: Atlas, 2015.

. Non-pecuniary reparation for moral damages. In: PAULA, Fernanda Pessoa Chauhy de; MENEZES, Iure Pedroza; and CAMPELLO, Nalva Cristina Barbosa (Coord.). *Rights of obligations: reflections on material and procedural law: work in honour of "Jones Figueiredo Alves".* Rio de Janeiro: Forense, 2011.

SILVESTRE, Gilberto Fachetti; HIBNER, Davi Amaral. The protection of personality rights in Brazil and Italy: material and procedural issues. In: *II Congress of International Civil Procedure - Proceedings of the II Congress of International Civil Procedure.* Vitória: UFES, 2017. v. 1. pp. 11-26.

SILVESTRE, Gilberto Fachetti; HIBNER, Davi Amaral; RAMALHO, Camila Vila Nova. Accessibility as a new personal right in Brazil: the Statute of Persons with Disabilities (Law 13.146/2015) and the moral damage that arises from inaccessibility - Spanish version. In: *Derecho PUCP - Revista de la Faculdad de Derecho da Pontifícia Universidad Católica del Peru,* v. 80, pp. 9-31, 2018.

; ; . Accessibility as a new personality right in Brazil: the Statute of Persons with Disabilities (Law 13.146/2015) and the moral damage resulting from inaccessibility - Portuguese version. In: *Derecho PUCP - Revista de la Faculdad de Derecho da Pontifícia Universidad Católica del Peru,* v. 80, pp. 9-30, 2018.

; ; . The civil liability of the company for the inaccessibility of the disabled person to the business establishment: material and procedural issues. In: *ARGUMENTUM (UNIMAR),* v. 18, pp. 731-758, 2017.

SPADONI, Joaquim Felipe. *Ação inibitória',* the action provided for in art. 461 of the CPC. 2ª ed. São Paulo: RT, 2007.

SZANIAWSKI, Elimar. *Personality rights and their protection.* 2ª Ed. São Paulo: Revista dos Tribunais, 2005.

TEPEDINO, Gustavo. Crisis of normative sources and legislative technique in the general part of the 2002 Civil Code. In: TEPEDINO, Gustavo (Coord.). *A parte geral do novo código civil:* estudos na perspectiva civil-constitucional. 2ª Ed. Rio de Janeiro: Renovar, 2003.

. *Civil Law Topics.* 4ª Ed. Rio de Janeiro: Renovar, 2008.

TOURINHO, Allan Veiga Brito; PERCY, Brenno Pires; OLIVEIRA, Camila Pereira; GASPAR, Ricardo Julio Dos Santos; MORAES, Rita De Cassia Monteiro. Evaluation of traffic conditions and accessibility on pavements. In: *Multidisciplinary Scientific Journal - Núcleo do Conhecimento.* Year 03, ed. 10, vol. 03, pp. 51- 63, October 2018.

VALIM, Rosangela Valim; TIOZZO, Arnaldo Ap. Acessibilidade: do direito a função social. In: *Pandora Brasil Magazine,* No. 26, January 2011.

WATANABE, Kazuo. Anticipatory relief and specific relief for obligations to do and not to do. In: TEIXEIRA, Sálvio de Figueiredo (coord.). *Reforma do Código de Processo Civil.* São Paulo: Saraiva, 2006.

ZARONI, Bruno Marzullo; PEREIRA, Paula Pessoa. Injunctive relief in the new CPC. In: DIDIER JR. Fredie; MACEDO, Lucas Buril de; PEIXOTO, Ravi; and FREIRE, Alexandre (Org.). *New CPC. Selected Doctrine.* Execution. Vol. 5. 2ª Ed. Salvador: JusPodivm, 2017.

Buy your books fast and straightforward online - at one of world's fastest growing online book stores! Environmentally sound due to Print-on-Demand technologies.

Buy your books online at
www.morebooks.shop

Kaufen Sie Ihre Bücher schnell und unkompliziert online – auf einer der am schnellsten wachsenden Buchhandelsplattformen weltweit! Dank Print-On-Demand umwelt- und ressourcenschonend produziert.

Bücher schneller online kaufen
www.morebooks.shop

Printed by Books on Demand GmbH, Norderstedt / Germany